ANOTHER AMERICA

THE POLITICS OF

RACE AND BLAME

KOFI BUENOR HADJOR

SOUTH END PRESS, BOSTON, MA

Library of Congress Catloging-in-Publication Data

Buenor Hadjor, Kofi
Another America: the politics of race and blame/ Kofi Buenor
Hadjor
p. cm.
Includes bibliographical references and index
ISBN 0-89608-515-5 (pbk.:alk.paper).
ISBN 0-89608-516-3 (cloth)
1. United States—Race relations. 2. Racism—United States. 3.
Afro-Americans—Social conditions—1975. 4. United
States—Social policy—1993.   I. Title.
E185.615.H235 1995
305.896'073—dc20

95-34269
CIP

South End Press, 116 St. Botolph Street, Boston, MA 02115

01 00 99 98 97 96 95   1 2 3 4 5 6 7 8 9

ANOTHER AMERICA

I dedicate this book to some special people who have meant so much to me in recent years:

My grandson, Jojo, and his soul cousins, Kyrah and Kwabena, in the hope that they grow to live in Dr. Martin Luther King Jr.'s world where they ARE judged by the content of their character and NOT by the color of their skin, a scenario that was not the case in my time.

Jojo's mother and my daughter, Dede, and his father, Guy, for the pleasure of having Jojo—the sunshine of my heart.

Jeanne and Jeffrey Levy-Hinte—the best friends that one could have.

CONTENTS

Acknowledgments..*vii*

Preface...ix

Chapter 1 - A Distorted Discourse..........................1

Chapter 2 - The Politics of Race..........................25

Chapter 3 - Blaming Blacks for Being Poor...........61

Chapter 4 - Crime: It's Always the Black Man.....89

Chapter 5 - The Invention of the Underclass.....123

Chapter 6 - The Black Response..........................155

Chapter 7 - Turning Things Around...................181

Notes...199

Bibliography..207

Index...213

About the Author...221

About South End Press..222

In memory of Elizabeth R. Harris

ACKNOWLEDGMENTS

I should like to thank the people whose perspectives and insights have helped me to shape and complete this book. In particular, I want to thank:

My colleagues and friends, professors Carlene Edie, Christopher McAuley, Claudine Michel, and Ula Taylor, who provided me with research help.

My student friends—Steve Houser, Kenyan Hunter, Joy Langford, David Leonard, and Kenee Shadbourne—who did the actual research.

The Department of Black Studies at UCSB for the administrative and secretarial support which was offered by Mimi Navarro and Carolyn Isono-Grapard;

Sylvia Curtis, the great Black Studies librarian at UCSB who got so much material for me for the book.

James Heartfield for allowing access to his work on "white flight" and the "underclass" debate and to Kevin Young for his insights on the gun control issue.

Ndugu Ali Mazrui and Mzee Immanuel Wallerstein for their intellectual support.

And Tarika Lewis, a great artist. To her, I say: "There will be another time, soon."

Pamela McAuley for her moral and spiritual support.

PREFACE

The primary goal of my adult life has been to further the goal of liberation. Thirty years ago I worked with Kwame Nkrumah and other leading anti-colonialists to create a new, free Africa from the ruins of the empire. Today, as an African living and working in California, I identify strongly with the struggle of Black Americans and other minorities to overcome inequality in this "civilized" nation. This book is intended as a small contribution toward advancing their cause, as they seek to achieve the liberation that is promised on paper to all in the United States of America.

I have paid close attention to the recent evolution of race relations in the United States, and have watched these relations developing in dangerously divisive directions. The only thing that surprised me about the Los Angeles riots of April 1992 was that they started so late and finished so soon. As I watch the daily news and listen to the opinions of people I encounter, I have become convinced that today, in racial terms, there truly are two Americas.

We have experienced a hardening of racial divisions in the United States. There has been an intensification of rivalries and conflicts among different racial and ethnic groups. Although this conflict may involve New York Jews or Los Angeles Koreans or Mexican immigrants, I believe that the basic, underlying divide is along Black and White lines. Blacks are not the only group to suffer racial discrimination and prejudice. Latinos and Asians have their own grim tales to tell. However, I believe that the Black/White divide is the keystone of racial conflicts in the United States, around which other intergroup tensions revolve. This is why I have chosen it as the primary focus of my argument. This racial divide has been badly exacerbated by the impact of economic decline and recession, which has made people more defensive about hanging onto whatever they have. All of these factors have increased the isolationary pressure on the have-nots. The group I am primarily concerned about in this book is poor Black communities.

Cultural expressions of the racial divide in modern America are all around us today. One has only to think of the most powerful trends in U.S popular music, which can often sound like the preparatory battle songs of an impending civil war. On one side, a rising country music star like Garth Brooks sings an anti-welfare song that gets the biggest cheer of his show from an overwhelmingly White, suburban, and small-town audience, which associates welfare with the Black urban "underclass." On the other side, the "gangsta" rap lyrics of artists like Snoop Doggy Dogg are identified with the violence and the lifestyles of the inner-city ghettos.

There are two Americas. But (apart from the odd appearance of a rapper on a music show) only one of them has an influential public voice that can be heard across the nation. This is the America that a congressman like Senator Bill Bradley of New Jersey claims to represent, when he complains about "young Black men, traveling in groups, cruising the city, looking for trouble," apparently ready to "snatch a purse, crash a concert, break open a telephone box," and maybe even to "rob a store, rape a jogger, shoot a tourist."[1]

The powerful elites at the top of American society have their platforms in Congress and television news studios. They have used those platforms to spread a message about "evil" in the Black ghettos of the inner cities, and to hold those pinned at the bottom of society responsible for many of the difficulties that the United States faces.

In the discussion dictated by U.S. power elites, reality has been turned upside down. Instead of talking about how society's problems affect Black people, the elites of U.S. politics and the media have focused attention on the false and poisonous notion that some Black people themselves are the problem. This idea is at the heart of a new post-liberal consensus that is emerging at the center of U.S. politics.

In the United States today, the controversial issue of race tends only to be discussed in coded terms, under the cover of a debate about other issues: taxation, law and order, family values. In general, the terms of the debate, dictated from the top down determine that these are all discussions which paint a dark and negative picture of Black communities. Reality is turned on its head, the truth is turned upside down, and some of the poorest and least powerful people in the United States become portrayed as the potent source of some of the major problems facing American society.

Politicians in Washington don't talk about the terrible things that racially distributed poverty is doing to the lives of Black communities in the inner cities. They talk more often about the problems caused to American society by Black people living on welfare. This pattern appears to hold true for just about all of the mainstream debates concerned with the position of impoverished Black people today.

Whether the talk is about there being too much crime and drugs in the ghetto or too many "illegitimate" children in poor Black households, the strong implication is always that Black people and their lifestyles are the biggest problem. This line of attack ends up depicting the behavior of a Black "underclass" as a major threat to social stability and the American way of life—an argument that, as we shall discuss later, is being used to criminalize entire generations of impoverished people in the inner cities of America.

Ask why most Black people get so little reward and so much repression in the United States today, and you are very likely to be informed that they have too much welfare, too much crime, and too many unwed mothers. If this line of argument continues to gain ground, how long will it be before the idea that there are simply too many poor Black people for America to cope with becomes an established wisdom of the political mainstream?

Indeed, the implicit assumption that there are too many poor blacks for America to handle is already being silently built into social policy. It is there in what looks like a groundbreaking campaign to try to limit numbers of unmarried Black mothers through a campaign to get inner-city teenagers to accept sterilizing implants in their arms. These methods appear to be only a step or two away from the kind of eugenicist forced-sterilization programs that have happened in the past in parts of the third world. But maybe that is appropriate, since many Black Americans seem likely to be living in urban shanty towns that are a kind of third world within the United States.

The assumption that there are too many blacks for America's good is there, too, in the policies of segregation and containment developed by the police and governmental agencies in U.S. cities such as New York, Washington, and Los Angeles. The permanent police road blocks and curfews in areas like South Central L.A., the racial red-lining in the best Whites-only suburbs, the shopping malls of the new fortress-styles city centers, where Black youths are stopped on sight by security guards—these features of American city life in the nineties are the components of a social, economic, and political system that treats the majority of Black people as a potential threat to public order and safety, which must be caged and kept at bay in order to protect the rest of society.

The assumption that blacks and other minorities are a threat to the rest of the United States is also there in contemporary political initiatives like the campaign to partition California. Listen to the words of Stan Statham, a legislator closely identified with the campaign for a separate State of Northern California. "I would like," says Statham, in his admirably blunt style, "to get rid of Los Angeles."* Partitioning California would involve formalizing the racial divide that has already been put in place informally, cutting off the impoverished millions in southern California from the rest of the state.

Statham used strong language to indicate his support of an independent northern California: "I would like to get rid of Los Angeles." Get rid of it! Take out the trash! It is as if the city's communities were garbage; a problem to be ditched, rather than people with problems that need to be addressed.

A worrying sign of where this scapegoating is headed can be seen in the way that the conservative elite turned illegal immigration into a major issue in the November 1994 congressional elections. The Republicans' argument that Latino hordes were sweeping over the border to enjoy the good life at the U.S. taxpayers' expense proved a resonant political focus for the unrest among White voters. The huge support for Proposition 187 in California, which proposed withholding basic welfare and educational services from undocumented immigrants, was a true sign of our times.

The campaign behind Proposition 187, was a masterpiece of political manipulation. First, the conservatives caused a budget and service crisis in California by cutting taxes and passing Proposition 13 to benefit the affluent. Then, they blamed the crisis on the penniless immigrants on the bottom of

---

* Stratham quoted on Channel 4 news (British Television), Jan. 19, 1993.

the social pile. Consevatives also managed to construct a consensus behind Proposition 187 that included everybody from
Republicans to members of the Green Party—and a fair number
of blacks who, in the twisted political climate of our age, were
persuaded that Latino immigrants were their competitors for
the crumbs from the White elite's table.

The anti-immigrant drive that took off in 1994 also provided evidence of the convergence of all sections of the political
elite around a post-liberal consensus on issues of race and
poverty. When Republican Governor Pete Wilson organized his
campaign advertisements around pictures of pandemonium at
the Tijuana/San Diego border checkpoint, the Democratic
Party's response was to call for more border patrols, and perhaps even the involvement of the National Guard, to keep the
Latino poor at bay.

By endorsing the notion that the Black and Latino poor are
largely responsible for their own plight and for some of the
broader problems facing U.S. society, the welfare-cutting
authorities have been able to do as they like. They have managed to shift much of the blame for the crisis in the U.S cities
onto those who have suffered from that crisis.

Many members of minority communities today have no
place in the U.S. political system. They have no high-powered
lobbyists to press their case in the corridors of power. They have
no expensive public-relations firms to sell their concerns to the
rest of the world, no tame newspaper lead-writers or television-
news anchormen to air their side of the story. They have no
silk-suited attorneys on hand to pursue defamation lawsuits
against those who slander them. In short, the way the political
system works today, they have no voice.

The main operators among the new generation of Black
politicians have not come forward to resolutely contest the
moral crusade against the "Black underclass" or the racially
loaded law-and-order crusade against "urban terrorism." As
spokespersons for the conservative "blacklash," some of these

politicians have been at the center of the call for an even tougher crackdown.

When Bill Clinton was elected president of the United States in November 1992, his message to the people was: "We're all in this together." There was to be no more divisive politics of "them" and "us." Instead, the United States would have to learn how to pull together as one, to rebuild prosperity and peace for all. Instead of division, the Clinton administration pledged to encourage "diversity." To many those sounded like fine words, and they seemed to be backed up by the appearance of numerous members of black, Latino, and other minority communities in high public office.

However, things out in the real world of U.S. race relations are very different from the rather rosy impression given by the inauguration rhetoric. But that would not be news to anybody who has to live in the inner cities of the United States, rather than in the rarified atmosphere occupied by President Clinton and his privileged "diverse" advisors. The real, underlying trend in American society today seems to be far less toward encouraging "diversity" than it is toward more enthusiastically endorsing racial *divergence* (also known as segregation).

What we are witnessing is not only a widening of the racial divide but also an increased differentiation between the treatment of different sections of the Black population. For a fortunate few members of the Black middle class, there may now be a more high-profile position at the center of U.S. affairs. At the same time, however, the vast majority of blacks in the United States are in danger of becoming even more isolated, more impoverished, and more harshly policed on the margins of U.S. economic and political life.

Washington may be opening its doors to more Black officials, spokespersons, lobbyists, columnists, and operators. But at the same time, the United States is seeking to slam the gates shut on the inner cities. The undeclared urban policy of containment is reaching a new level of intensity, as the authorities take steps to wall off the inner-city ghettos from the rest of the United States, both physically and morally, as if they were some sort of netherworld.

The endorsement of "diversity" in public life means that a relative handful of Black and Latino attorneys-turned-officials are being allowed to move closer toward the center of U.S. affairs. Meanwhile, the majority of Black and Latino communities are being shoved further out towards the margins. What we are witnessing is the creation of an *illusion* of increased representation and empowerment for Black and Latino people, an illusion which masks the fact that these people are having their marginal influence in American society further eroded.

The much-vaunted culture of diversity and rise of the Black middle class have proved just about useless in responding to the politics of racial scapegoating. They offer no effective defense to ordinary Black people in a situation where all the evidence suggests things are going to get worse rather than better.

The authorities at every level of government are seeking to slash spending on welfare, healthcare, and education for the poor. The police in every city in the United States are gearing up with new strong-arm methods and technology to contain the ghettos. The moral crusade that seems to blame the "Black underclass" for its own problems is reaching a new pitch of intensity. The "war against welfare" now commands a new consensus of support across the political spectrum, including influential voices within the new middle-class leadership of the Black community itself.

There is a desperate need today to start turning things around, to give a voice to the interests of those who are trapped, silently, at the bottom of society and scapegoated for so much of what is wrong in the United States today. The first and most important thing that needs to be said at every opportunity is that the Black poor and their behavior are not responsible for the problems facing the country today.

"To engage in a serious discussion of race in America, we must begin not with the problems of Black people but with the flaws of American society—flaws rooted in historic inequalities and long-standing cultural stereotypes."* I believe that Cornel West, a well-known black intellectual, is absolutely correct to identify looking at U.S. society as the starting point of any serious debate.

The problems that need to be addressed are social problems dealing with the way that society functions, rather than the way that Black, Latino, or any other individuals behave. However, many of these social problems afflict Black people disproportionately.

State repression and injustice, discrimination and deprivation are fundamental problems that need to be tackled as pressing priorities. They are the major negative experiences shaping life for many Black Americans. By tackling them, we will also find a key to address the more sensational problems of life in the inner cities, such as drug-related crime and violence, upon which media and political attention is far too narrowly focused.

Underlying this discussion is another widely accepted notion that needs to be overturned: the belief that it is wrong to talk openly about race in U.S. politics. It is important that the United States begins to discuss openly the issue of race and the attitudes of those in authority, and of society as a whole towards the issue of race.

In particular, issues of race cannot continue to be buried beneath a blanket of other, mystifying issues. It is time that all of the ciphers and codes used in U.S. politics were broken. The double-meaning discussions about the problems of crime or welfare are being exposed for what they really are: largely moralistic attempts to scapegoat the poor, especially the Black poor, for the problems of the cities and for wider social malaise.

---

* Cornel West, *Race Matters*, Beacon Press, Boston, 1993, p.3.

The issue of race and the reality of what Black people put up with in this country ought to replace these dishonest debates.

In this spirit, it is vital, too, that critically minded people should participate in and challenge the terms of the discussions about "the problem of the Black 'underclass.'" As argued elsewhere in this book, the central problem to be addressed is not some behavioral "culture of poverty" but poverty itself among Blacks and Latinos in the inner cities.

Tackling the dire economic circumstances of these communities should be of paramount importance. In the first place, this focus will involve challenging elitists ideas and the arguments that are routinely used in an effort to explain away Black poverty—primarily the various reactionary theories that center on the existence of a criminal "Black underclass," which has been accused of creating its own problems, and most of society's problems too.

My intention in writing this book is to help begin the process of dismantling the ideological walls that are used to trap many blacks in poverty, and to expose the manipulative discourse on race. This discourse allows the U.S. political and economic elites to escape responsibility for the problems of their system. The task of challenging their case is only just beginning. It is vital that it be pursued if we are to give a voice to the dispossessed and point the finger at the real source of the insecurities and divisions which, ultimately, distort all of our lives in the United States today.

The issue is not how Black people can be turned into decent Americans. It is how American society can be made decent enough for all of us to live in.

Kofi Buenor Hadjor
Department of Black Studies
University of California,
Santa Barbara, July 1995

1. A DISTORTED DISCOURSE

More than at any time since the Civil War, the United States is today a nation divided against itself. Intergroup tensions, which have long festered beneath the surface of American society, now come bubbling to the surface with increasing regularity and intensity. Whatever the immediate cause of a particular conflict might appear to be, in most cases the underlying focus of contention is the issue of race.

The disuniting of the United States is a dangerous development that poses serious problems for the future of this society. If we are to work towards a solution, the first questions that have to be answered are these: what is behind the division, and what forces are responsible for making the racial divide the most pressing issue of our time?

Of course, the divisions in America today do not usually present themselves in the form of an open race war. The tensions and conflicts are most often mediated and expressed through other, less controversial categories. The public battle lines are drawn as a contest for resources and influence between the suburbs and the cities, or between the taxpayers and the welfare dependents, or between the law-abiding, moral citizens and the deviant "underclass." However, as we shall see throughout our analysis, most of these categories are simply operating as code words for the underlying racial divide, and are widely understood as such.

The extent to which most people implicitly understand the Black-and-White code in which racial politics are presented has been borne out by recent election results across the United States. In key areas, millions of voters now line up along clear racial lines. The Republican Party's landslide success in the November 1994 congressional elections demonstrated this development to a startling degree. In the previous three elections for the House of Representatives, White voters had split 50/50 between Democrats and Republicans. In November 1994, the percentage split was a huge 58/42 in favor of the GOP. On the others side of the divide, an overwhelming 88 percent of Black voters stayed with the Democrats.[1] Meanwhile, the furious row over illegal immigrants, focused around the passage of Proposition 187 in California, gave an added dimension to the race issue in those elections and beyond.

The problem of the divided society is now widely recognized across the political spectrum. Politicians and commentators of varying perspectives have been forced to address, at least rhetorically, the deepening intergroup differences and tensions within the social fabric of the United States. The responses that many influential voices have so far come up with, however, are almost as dangerous as the racial divisions themselves. A new post-liberal consensus is emerging, one that effectively holds the Black poor responsible for intensifying racial tensions by alienating themselves from mainstream American society.

There has been an important shift of emphasis in the discourse about the Black poor in America over the past 25 to 30 years. In the sixties, discrimination and social inequality were widely recognized as the most pressing issues. Government was held responsible to society as a whole to do something about these problems. Those in government, acting as the agents of society, were expected to act, through the social and economic policies of the Great Society and the War on Poverty, to help overcome divisions and facilitate equality. In the nineties, however, things appear very different.

The discourse on race relations now emphasizes, not the failings of the political and economic system, but the failings of individual Blacks and members of other minorities. It is widely argued that, through their own "underclass" behavior patterns and ghetto culture, Black people have created many of their own problems of poverty and communal degradation, and by so doing, have distanced themselves from other sections of the American population. Interracial tensions are now commonly ascribed not to *social* factors, that is, as the consequences of the way that society is managed, but to *cultural* or *behavioral* differences and defects among different racial groups. As we shall see, some commentators and analysts have even gone so far as to reintroduce the long-discredited concept of *natural* differences among Blacks and Whites.

In most of the current discourse, the existence of a top-down system of racial discrimination and elite domination has been entirely removed from the picture. Insofar as racism is recognized as a continuing problem within the framework of the post-liberal consensus, it is seen as an *attitudinal* problem, relating to the backward prejudices of certain sections of the public, rather than as an *institutional* force produced by the dominant power relations in society.

Divorced from any notion of systematic discrimination, attitudinal racism is held to be a problem that can be found as readily among certain types of Black people as among White. In either case, it is apparently something that originates and festers at the bottom of society. Accuse those at the top of perpetuating racism today, and they will simply throw up their hands and say that they have been forced to go along with the pressure of popular prejudice from below. Thus newspaper editors will insist that they concentrate on lurid stories of Black crime because that is what their readers demand, while politicians will claim that their clamp-down on immigration or their latest assault on welfare payments to single mothers in the ghetto are only a response to the demands of their constituents for tough action against these groups. The powerful elites are strangely powerless to resist the tide of racially charged opinion from below, or so their apologists would have us believe.

This book's intervention in the debate about race in America today is to challenge the assumptions on which too much of this discourse is currently based. The starting point for our critique is that the recent trend in the race discourse is contradictory and problematic in two important ways. First, it blames those on the receiving end of discrimination for creating racial divisions and enhancing their own inequality. And second, it treats racism as a problem of the masses, instead of a political device of the social and political elites.

Through the "underclass" debate, the Black and minority communities of the inner cities are being held responsible for the inequalities and racial tensions from which they suffer. And worse yet, they are also being blamed for many of the biggest problems facing American society today, from crime to the government budget deficit. The reality is, however, the other way around. Racial discrimination and intergroup divisions are an intrinsic product of the way in which society itself is organized. And the politics of race-hate, far from being a spontaneous product from below, have been perpetuated and often manipulated by elite groups at the top of American society, which have ruthlessly exploited racially loaded ideologies and policies in order to help protect their own power and privileges.

It is our contention here that the Black urban "underclass," so often blamed for problems such as poverty, crime, and family breakdown, has in fact been set up by America's elites as both a symbol of and a scapegoat for the decay of American society today.

The "underclass" is a symbol of social malaise, inasmuch as all of the elite's insecurities about the future of America have been displaced onto the rotting ghettos of the inner cities, which now represent damning evidence of America's failure to fulfill its dream. And at the same time, the "underclass" is a scapegoat for this social malaise because, by focusing on the moral short-comings of ghetto communities as the cause of that poverty and decay, the elites are able to shift attention away from the serious shortcomings in their management of the economic and political system.

In this way, much of the race discourse today can be seen as an old-fashioned exercise in blaming the poor and the powerless for the nation's difficulties, and so letting the powerful off the hook. What is new is that this prejudice is now wrapped up in the sociological jargon of the "underclass" debate and, as such, is given far greater credence by liberal critics.

The hidden reality is that the basic cause of rising inter-group tensions in the United States has little to do with cultural or behavioral factors. It rests upon the failure of the American social and economic systems to integrate millions of Blacks and other minorities into a successful order. The statistical proof of that failure to integrate is not hard to find, for those who wish to seek it out. As Andrew Hacker's impressive statistical study of discrimination has shown, for example, on average Black families earned just $580 for every $1000 earned by White families in 1990.[2] Beneath the surface of the debates about culture clashes and ethnic tensions, this is the nub of the problem of race relations in contemporary American society. The intergroup divisions are essentially based upon the unequal relationship that different racial groups enjoy to the centers of economic, social, and political power, and upon the struggle for resources and for the access to influence which results.

From the point of view of those at the top of the pecking order, the beauty of the contemporary discourse on race is that it legitimizes their system's failure to help prosper and to integrate the Black minority, by pointing the finger of blame at the impoverished Blacks themselves and emphasizing the doctrine of individual responsibility.

Today's political and intellectual discourse on race does not only deny the responsibility of institutionalized discrimination for the problems facing Black communities. Insofar as it acknowledges the existence of racism in the 1990s, it distorts the dynamic that is behind racial thinking, by treating it as a problem that comes from the bottom of society upwards. It is our contention, by contrast, that the impetus behind the power of racial ideas in American society comes from the top downwards.

Racial politics serve the interests of the powerful elites that control most of the clout and wealth in the United States. In the past, encouraging intergroup tensions has often helped these elites to disaggregate any popular opposition. More recently, the coded anti-Black messages that have often topped the political agenda, around issues such as taxation or crime, have helped to consolidate a constituency for conservatism—a particularly valuable asset in the post-Cold War era, when the collapse of the old enemy, communism, had left the Right with little to mobilize against. An institutionalized system of racial double-standards has supplied the elites with an effective excuse for their failure to tackle problems such as poverty or unemployment. And at the same time, it has given them a powerful justification for using hard-line policing methods to control those minorities whom the failure to integrate has excluded from the mainstream and confined to the margins of America's economic and social life.

To insist that racial politics are a device of the American elites is not to deny that there is such a thing as popular racism. Of course there is. But the question we seek to address in this book is, by what process do such anti-Black prejudices arise, and what gives them particular force and popular resonance in specific periods of time?

If grassroots racism among White Americans were simply an outburst of irrational prejudice, there is no reason why it should assume more importance than other prejudices such as, say, a dislike of people with ginger hair. But race-hate is not simply an irrational prejudice. It is rooted in the realities of American society. Many White people are prepared to treat Blacks as inferior, second-class citizens because, in the workings of the American economic and social system, Blacks generally *are* second-class citizens. It is the reality of institutionalized discrimination that gives racial division such a potent meaning in the popular imagination.

That race-hate should acquire a particular public presence or intensity at times is no accident either. Once it has been implanted in the public consciousness by the way society is run along segregated lines, the racial divide can readily be politicized, usually to serve the interests of the ruling elite. Thus the genuine insecurities that many White people feel in the uncertain economic climate of America today have been displaced onto racially loaded issues, but only after being channelled through the ideological focus created by the dominant political and media interests. The relationship between elite ideologies and popular racism is a complex and dynamic one. But it is a pretty sure bet that the real force behind the use and abuse of racial issues always comes from the top downwards.

THE ISSUE OF OUR TIMES

It is of vital importance that the institutional and top-down character of racism should be more widely understood today. The distortions that currently surround race-related issues are having a major impact on how many problems are perceived in the United States of America at the end of the twentieth century.

In the first instance, there is the creation and perpetuation of a system of segregated living space that has elsewhere been aptly described as "American apartheid."[3] As we shall argue in later chapters, institutional racism has built and continually reinforces this system through the consolidation of inner-city economic ghettos for Black and other minority communities, alongside the encouragement of the "White flight" to the suburbs. And the current discourse on race has legitimized this system of American apartheid, by holding the Black poor responsible for their problems in the ghetto and describing the White flight as a spontaneous attempt to escape from the urban criminal "underclass."

U.S. politics, too, is seriously affected by the distorted way in which race-related issues are perceived today. Antagonism towards the cities, and their supposed "underclass" populations of Black welfare queens, criminals, and drug pushers, has become the bedrock of a post-liberal consensus that now bridges the approach of all parties to all issues. Coded, racially loaded issues like welfare, taxes, and crime have been at the cutting edge of the conservative wedge that has largely driven traditional liberalism off the political map and forced the Democrats to make their peace with a Republican agenda over the past 25 years or so.

The arena of social policy provides perhaps the clearest evidence of the impact that the distorted perceptions of race-related issues are having in America today. Through the focus on dealing with the immoral or criminally inclined Black "underclass," the priorities of social policy have been completely rewritten. Any notion of trying to build a better society through investing in communities is out. Now the emphasis is on the need to contain those portrayed as an incorrigibly antisocial section of society. The result is the preoccupation with law-and-order politics that we see today. The United States is now a society in which "a decade of right-wing crime policy has made imprisonment the fastest-growing program of government" and where the Justice Department could report in October 1994 that "The nation's prison population has now passed one million, triple the level of 1980—with no measurable impact on public safety."[4]

There has been a fundamental shift in the accepted understanding of the causes of inequality and difference among racial groups over the past 30 years. It is this shift towards a more conservative climate of debate which acts to legitimize much that is wrong today. In order to show how this works, we will briefly outline the development of the discourse about racial inequality and tensions over the past three decades, and then focus at some length on the arguments of a groundbreaking study that can be seen as the culmination of this process: Charles Murray's *The Bell Curve*. Published in 1994, Murray's book claims that inherent IQ differences between racial groups can explain their different standing in society. The fact that a widely respected academic like Murray could seriously propose such an argument today—and that the liberal response should be so ineffective and unsure—symbolizes the mood of our times, as far as the discourse about race and equality is concerned.

FROM KERNER TO MURRAY

In *Dark Ghetto*, written in 1965, Kenneth B. Clark outlined a view of the relationship between American society and its Black minority which now sounds incredibly radical, but which, in response to the inner-city riots of the mid-sixties, was to be widely accepted:

"The dark ghetto's invisible walls have been erected by the White society, by those who have power, both to confine those who have NO power and to perpetuate their powerlessness. The dark ghettos are social, political, educational, and above all, educational colonies. Their inhabitants are subject peoples, victims of the greed, cruelty, insensitivity, guilt and fear of their masters."[5]

Official recognition of the importance of discrimination and segregation in the creation of the "race problem" came in 1968, with the publication of the Kerner Commission's report into causes of urban violence. America, concluded Kerner, was becoming two societies: Black and White, "separate and unequal," thanks to the systematic discrimination and segregation that had become a threat to "the future of every American."[6] The Kerner Commission was in no doubt as to where the responsibility for the widening racial rift lay:

"What White Americans have never fully understood—but what the Negro can never forget—is that White society is deeply implicated in the ghetto. White institutions created it, White institutions maintain it, and White society condones it."[7]

In which case, the Commission argued, U.S. society had a responsibility to do something about it, by both investing in the inner cities and encouraging policies that would enhance the integration of the Black minority into the mainstream.

This essentially *social* explanation of the problems relating to race and poverty in the United States became the predominant view of the moment. But it was not the only one. Already, the notion was being propagated that the cultural characteristics and behavior of impoverished Blacks themselves were at least partly responsible for the problem. Thus Oscar Lewis coined the phrase "Culture of Poverty" as early as 1965, and by 1967 Daniel P. Moynihan was reporting on what he termed "a tangle of pathology" within ghetto Black communities.[8]

Writers like these did try to connect the societal problems of unemployment and discrimination to the creation of a culture of poverty. But they also made a crucial concession to the conservatives, insisting that, once established, the culture of poverty could take on a life of its own, disconnected from any problems caused by wider economic and social trends or government policies. As liberalism retreated through the seventies and eighties, this concession was to help pave the way for the rewriting of the textbooks. The emphasis steadily shifted away from explanations that held social and institutional factors responsible for the crisis in the ghettos and towards those which pointed the finger of blame at the cultural and moral norms—or alleged lack of them—among impoverished Blacks.

By the early and mid-eighties, the additional factor thrown into the pot by conservative academics like Charles Murray and Lawrence Mead was the attempt to blame government welfare policies for the perpetuation of the ghetto.[9] The problem with welfare was no longer seen as the pitifully low standard of living it provided, which trapped those receiving it at the bottom of the pile. Now the problem the experts saw with welfare was that it was somehow too generous and too easily accessible, so that it discouraged the poor from taking jobs or raising "proper" families and allowed them to indulge in their own deviant lifestyles. This interpretation now became the predominant viewpoint through which social policy was developed and assessed. Within the space of 20 years, social intervention in support of the Black communities of the ghetto had turned from being seen as the potential solution to one of the major ills of American society to being widely perceived as the cause of the problem.

It is important to emphasize here that what changed over the years was the intellectual and political climate in which issues of race and poverty were discussed. The reality of high unemployment, bad housing, and desperate poverty in the inner cities has not altered substantially. What has changed beyond recognition is the *perception* of these problems that now dominates public discourse. It is the shift in the balance of political power and the creation of a post-liberal consensus within the elites of American society that explains these developments, rather than anything that might actually have happened within the Black communities of the inner-city districts.

The theoretical and intellectual shift towards holding the Black poor responsible for their own problems was taken one stage further in 1994, with the publication of *The Bell Curve*, written by Charles Murray and co-author Richard Herrnstein (who incidently died before the book's publication). It is well worth examining the arguments of *The Bell Curve* and the responses to it at some length, not because they necessarily warrant it in their own terms, but because they provide perhaps the most dramatic available snapshot of the way that irrational and dangerous ideas can now have an increasingly influential bearing on the debate about race and social policy in the United States, a bearing of the sort that demands a concerted response.

AN UNINTELLIGENT ARGUMENT

The publication of the book *The Bell Curve: Intelligence and Class Structure in American Life* sparked a major intellectual controversy. Its authors claim that cognitive ability, as measured in Intelligence Quotient (IQ) tests, is an inherited trait that substantially accounts for inequalities in wealth, income and education.

The claim that some races are naturally superior to others was once upheld as a principle of both science and common sense by the ruling elites of all western societies. In the early years of the twentieth century, U.S. President Theodore Roosevelt could publicly justify a war fleet to the Pacific to warn off Japanese emigrants on the grounds that "we have to build up our Western country with our White civilization."[10] However, in more recent times, the idea of innate racial superiority has been taboo ever since Nazi racial policies led to the Holocaust. Charles Murray and Richard Herrnstein have effectively broken that taboo in their book, *The Bell Curve*.

At the heart of the controversy over the Bell Curve is a correlation between tested IQ, income, and race. According to Murray and Herrnstein, "Wages earned by people in high-IQ occupations have pulled away from the wages in low-IQ occupations, and differences in education cannot explain most of this change."[11] As a comment on diverging incomes, this is not a controversial finding. It is now widely accepted that throughout the last 15 years in the United States, those with high incomes have seen their wages rise still higher, while those with low incomes have lost out even more.

A variety of authors, from former Nixon advisor Kevin Phillips to Labor Secretary Robert Reich, have demonstrated that the free-market policies of the Reagan/Bush years only led to greater social division. The problem that conservatives face is how to explain the failure of the free market to bring prosperity. The virtue of *The Bell Curve* for them is in the use of IQ to explain divisions in American society. If income inequalities are due to natural differences, then no blame attaches to the market economy. The rich are rich because it is in their makeup to succeed, just as it is the lot of the poor to fail. In this way, an emphasis upon individual IQ can serve as an apology for the failure of an economic system.

The apologetic character of IQ is even more marked in the case of race. It is bad enough for the free market, with its boasts of equality and freedom, that there are winners and losers, but all of the evidence points to the fact that the winners are predominantly White and the biggest losers are Black. A wealth of recent material demonstrates that Black Americans have lost out to such an extent as to make a mockery of free enterprise, and that the gap between Black and White incomes, if anything, widened between 1979 and 1990.[12] According to *The Bell Curve*, the failure of American Blacks to close the income gap is due not to discrimination, but to their lower average intelligence as measured in IQ tests. Murray and Herrnstein cite findings that Black Americans are on average 15 percentage points below the average IQ. The clear implication is that the innate stupidity of Blacks, not discrimination in the labor market, is responsible for their social inferiority.

Murray and Herrnstein go further. They look at Black performance in education, employment, and income, but adjust the unequal figures to take into account lower IQ. At the end of this process, they manage to estimate that Black students of average IQ have a 68 percent chance of getting a degree, higher than the 50 percent chance of Whites. And they estimate that Blacks of average IQ have a 26 percent chance of getting into a "high IQ occupation," while equally intelligent Whites have only a 10 percent chance.

The message here is dramatic. By adjusting the figures to take into account lower-tested IQ, *The Bell Curve* not only eliminates the difference in income, but suggests that in employment and education, Blacks are privileged. As Murray and Herrnstein argue, "… the evidence presented here should give everyone who writes and talks about ethnic inequalities reason to avoid flamboyant rhetoric about ethnic oppression."[13] By introducing IQ into the equation, the authors exonerate the U.S. market economy of racial discrimination: Blacks fail because they are less intelligent. Indeed, these estimates support Murray's argument that the real discrimination is in favor of Blacks, through affirmative action.

If social and racial inequalities really can be explained in terms of natural differences, it would present a powerful defense against the accusation that the free market has failed. The problem is, however, that *The Bell Curve*'s case does not stand up under any scrutiny. Murray's is a sloppy, unintelligent argument. Yet it has succeeded in disconcerting many liberals and putting a new slant on the race discourse. These effects are a telling sign of how far the terms of the debate have shifted against Black people. To emphasize the extent to which this process signifies the contemporary collapse of liberalism, rather than any power of conservative ideologies, let us look at just how shoddy the case contained in *The Bell Curve* really is.

Murray and Herrnstein cannot claim to have identified any definite link between tested IQ and any natural feature, but that does not stop them from suggesting that one will turn up. Writing of ethnic differences in IQ, they say that these "may well include some (as yet unknown) genetic component" (their parentheses) and "The evidence may eventually become unequivocal that genes are part of the story."[14]

The whole edifice of their 845-page book is built upon a statistical correlation between tested IQ, social status, and race. But statistical correlations prove nothing. At best, they can indicate a connection, but the theory that the connection is a natural inheritance remains unproven, despite the best efforts of racial thinkers down the centuries.

The first and basic point to insist upon in response to Murray's argument is that the real explanation of inequalities is to be found not at the level of individual intelligence or attributes of some other sort, but at the level of society as a whole. Differences in income, occupation, and education are generated as a consequence of the different relationships that individuals and groups have to the process of creating and controlling wealth in society.

Throughout the free-market eighties, income inequality widened as a consequence of the differential impact of economic boom and recession on different classes and groups. The peculiarly marginal position of American Blacks to production ensures that they will pay the heaviest price for the re-emergence of recession. Those inequalities have been systematically reproduced by the inability of a stagnant market economy to fully integrate Black labor into society. Of all the ethnic groups in America, only Blacks are defined by their marginalization from the production process.

This brings us to the second and more complex point. If the weakness of the market economy accounts for social and racial inequalities, what are we to make of the differences in tested IQ between people of different classes and races? The general "not-in-front-of-the-children" response to *The Bell Curve* from the social-sciences establishment seemed to suggest that perhaps we should not mention such embarrassing matters at all. But the argument has to be dealt with. In fact, it should come as no surprise that people lower down on the social ladder *should* score worse at IQ tests. Whatever the finer points of intelligence tests, the hard fact is that those with greater social power will tend to score higher.

Critics of IQ tests prefer to sidestep this issue by arguing that the tests carry a cultural bias in favor of the White middle classes. They point out that IQ test questions have often presumed knowledge of things, like sailing regattas, that are the narrow preserve of the well-heeled. IQ tests do tend to reflect the values and standards of the societies that produce them. For instance, one test set in Nazi Germany asked examinees to formulate a sentence containing the words "war...soldier...nation." There is an interesting debate to be had about the efficacy of standardized IQ tests for assessing people from varying backgrounds. But in the interests of testing the arguments, let us assume for the moment a worst-case scenario. Let's say that Murray and Herrnstein are right to say that IQ tests reflect intelligence. All that proves is the impact of social inequality, not of natural difference.

Intelligence is shaped by an individual's relation to and experience of interacting in society. Those, like Blacks in America, who are marginal to society are prevented from participating in the decisionmaking that stimulates what Herrnstein and Murray call "cognitive ability." Relegated to ghetto life, underemployment, and few chances of social mobility, you just have fewer opportunities to get your wits stretched.

Contrary to the evidence of a racial basis to intelligence, the U.S. military discovered after the World War II that Whites from the rural South scored lower on IQ tests than Blacks from the industrial North; thus the impoverished South proved to be an even worse environment for the development of intelligence than the city ghettos of the North. In general, the bias is in society, not in the wording of the tests.

If, as *The Bell Curve* argues, intelligence were fixed, that would be bad news for Blacks as well as for Whites with low incomes and low IQ scores. In that case, social position, too, would be fixed. However, intelligence is much more malleable than Murray and Herrnstein admit.

First of all, IQ scores overall rise with the passing of time. The convention of making the average IQ at any one time equal to 100 masks the fact that the average tested IQ has risen by 15 points since the World War II. But rising IQs should come as no surprise. Each generation is better educated and more worldly-wise than the last. Travel and mass media make our knowledge of the world a lot more comprehensive than our grandparents.

Secondly, individual IQs are, against all genetic argu-ments, remarkably susceptible to intervention. People whose circumstances change radically often become radically different themselves. No one wonders at the speed with which some young Asian immigrants can change their accents and their tastes once in America. All sorts of influences and experiences, at home or work, through the media and among friends, can work to make you a different person.

The Bell Curve cites the case of the Head Start program of intensive nursery-level education for children from poor back-grounds. They point out that while Head Start can increase recorded IQs by as much as ten points at the beginning of the program, the gain tends to fade out over time. As they see it, natural intelligence wins out over special assistance. However, what the fade-out of the initial gain in IQ really shows, is how the experience of the real world imposes limits on the effective-ness of policy intervention in the classroom. Special encourage-ment can bear results at first, but before long children caatch onto the fact that a bit of extra schooling does not mean that they are going to escape from the ghetto. Rundown schools and brothers and sisters out of work all confirm the realistic expec-tations of children and parents about future opportunities. A small amount of pre-school encouragement is soon knocked out of any promising students by the grim reality of the U.S public school system.

The whole purpose of the education system is to make people cleverer than they were. Often people who get a chance to pick up their education late in life are amazed by the change of their outlook. People pushed by their parents to pursue the college education unavailable to that earlier generation cringe with embarrassment when introducing an unsophisticated mom or dad to friends. College life, the migration from home, the new social contacts and independence can make even the most parochial provincial boy into something like an urban sophisticate. The fact that the vast majority of Black people in the United States are denied the opportunity to expand their experiences and education in this way has obvious and far-reaching implications for their IQ scores.

Murray and Herrnstein's case for a naturally determined intelligence is, for the most part, a justification of the status quo. To that end, the authors warn against attempts to buck the genetic market with positive discrimination and any excessive resourcing of lower education. But that does not mean they really want to see a laissez-faire education policy. Instead, the authors of The Bell Curve want additional spending on "gifted children"—as if the education system were not already a substantial subsidy to the middle class. Privilege, not equality of opportunity, is the message of the genetic intelligence argument.

The argument of The Bell Curve defends the market against the charge of failing Blacks and the poor and promoting privilege. It is a transparent display of prejudice and double standards, dressed up in the language of social pseudo-science. The fact that such notions can now seriously be put forward by somebody other than far-right cranks, and can attract national and international attention, is a most telling sign of how far the conservative arguments on race, class, and poverty in the United States have now travelled. The response that The Bell Curve received from its critics is equally instructive, as an insight into the collapse of traditional liberalism before the new elitist ideologies, which now dominate and distort the discourse about race, the "underclass," and American society.

ELITISM, OLD AND NEW

The Bell Curve did not receive a favorable reaction from the middle-class intelligentsia whose corner it argues. Instead, it was the highbrow press, from *Newsweek* to the *New Republic*, that most violently attacked *The Bell Curve*, even to the extent of arguing that it should be banned. The content of their criticisms, however, provides a useful guide to the state of liberal opinion in the nineties.

Most of the writers published in the *New Republic* issue devoted to *The Bell Curve* did not argue that social privilege must be challenged at its roots and reject *The Bell Curve* as an apologia for elitism. Instead, the principle argument against *The Bell Curve* in the broadsheets and the glossies seemed to be that it had drawn attention to the unequal achievements of Black people and White people living in the United States. The voices of educated liberalism were not really concerned to take apart the reactionary, racially loaded content of what Murray and Herrnstein had said. Rather, their essential response was to protest, "You cannot say that!" It was as if, with the exhaustion of the old liberal agenda on social policy, they had no arguments left to offer against the conservative case, other than to protest in embarrassment that the controversial and divisive arguments put forward in *The Bell Curve* should not be allowed to see the light of day.

Typical of the *New Republic* responses, for example, Alan Wolfe wondered what the difference is "between thinking that the Black male beside me is dumb and thinking that there's a 25 percent chance he's dumb," a parody of *The Bell Curve*'s probability approach. Wolfe is addressing not the real issue of the inequality between him and the Black male but the question of public etiquette. His expressed concern seems to be less about tackling the reality of racial division than about avoiding the possibility of adding the insult of bad thoughts to the injury of inequality.[15]

Behind the hysterical calls for bans, the liberal response to the substance of *The Bell Curve*'s arguments was noticeably mealy-mouthed and ineffective, reflecting the shift in the terms of the discourse on race and U.S. society. The argument that inequalities are not the responsibility of the U.S. system has been won, albeit in many cases by default. The post-liberal consensus now accepts that the explanation for the problems faced by the Black poor must largely be found, not in the power structures at the top of U.S. society, but within the attributes of that racial group itself. That is a respectable, mainstream view today.

The objection to *The Bell Curve*'s argument was generally only that it framed its elitist arguments too much in the language of the past. Up-front racism with a eugenic framework is pretty alien to today's intelligentsia. Murray and Herrnstein's mistake is to resurrect the traditional racism of 60 years ago.

Today, the poverty of the Black inner cities is not the source of racial pride for the elite—in the way that the domination of the European empires over the world was in the past—but a symbol of social decay. Contemporary elitist thinking rarely draws explicit attention to color, as *The Bell Curve* does. Instead, the middle class's sense of superiority is articulated around moral issues, like family structure, legitimacy, and crime. The irony is that in the past, Charles Murray's investigations of the underclass suited those prejudices well and have become increasingly influential across the political spectrum.

The new elitism accepts the argument of people like Charles Murray that the "underclass" and its culture of poverty are responsible for the crisis in U.S. cities and for many problems facing the wider U.S. society. But its case against the Black poor is framed in the modern code, rather than the explicitly racial language of the past. The emphasis is on moral and cultural problems and differences, rather than racial inferiority. *The Bell Curve* attracted flak for overstepping the mark and breaking the race taboo. But the essence of its argument—that the Black "underclass" is stuck at the bottom of the pile for reasons which have nothing to do with the way U.S. society is managed—is now the starting point for the race discourse as a whole. That is a chilling sign of just how far the terms of the debate have shifted, of how far the truth about racial discrimination has been turned on its head. It is that above all which has inspired this book, as an attempt to help turn things around.

A SOCIAL CONSTRUCT

The argument that needs to be repeated—in a thousand different ways, at every juncture in the intellectual exchange over race—is that, contrary to the assumptions underpinning the current discourse, racial differences and inequalities are *not* the product of natural, cultural, or behavioral factors. Instead, racial differences are a social and political construction.

The fact that people's skins are of different color needs have no more bearing on their place in the world than the difference in the color of their hair or eyes. Race has been turned into a more significant force only by the pressure of contemporary social facts—that is, by the operations of the economic and social system that has failed to achieve equality or integration, and by the interventions of self-serving elites who have seen fit to politicize racial issues and differences, so as to enhance their own authority and control over others.

When arguing that race is a social, rather than natural, construction, we face, however, one more trap that needs to be avoided, one more imbalance in the current discussion of racial issues that we need to correct.

In a reaction against the attempt by conservatives to "naturalize" racial differences and inequalities, some insightful academics working in post-colonial studies have sought to develop an alternative analysis of race as a phenomenon that has been socially constructed, usually by powerful elites. This represents an important advance. The historical investigations of the ideologies and institutions of White supremacy, in books such as David Roediger's *Towards the Abolition of Whiteness* and Theodore Allen's *Invention of the White Race*, are often superb. Here, racial division is not excused as something naturally given but critically examined as an artificial constraint that serves to make real inequalities.[16]

However, the narrow way that the new school of social constructionists has developed theories of race poses new problems. Despite their emphasis on the "social" origins of race, these writers rarely examine how racial divisions are produced and reproduced by the way in which society is organized. Instead, they tend to concentrate on the ideological and institutional demarcations thrown up by racial groups themselves. The relation between the social divisions created by an economic and social system and the strength of racial feeling is obscured, as racism is reduced to the ideas, prejudices, and actions of individuals.

This dispute over the interpretation of race as a social construct has important implications. If we believe that the roots of racial thinking lie in the way that society is organized from the top down, it follows that combating racial divisions will require reorganizing society itself. By contrast, many of the new theories of race as a social construction see racism as principally a prejudice. The conclusion that this points to is that racism can be challenged by building a Black counterculture, by encouraging a sort of alternative version of a subjectively constructed identity. Promoting many different cultures in this way may well strike a blow against the notion that one group is superior; but it can also end up excusing and reinforcing racial divisions in a language that is far more acceptable today than the old ideologies of White supremacy.

Race *is* a social and political construction, and if that insight were developed to its full potential, it would be a powerful weapon against those who claim racial differences and inequalities are natural or unavoidable. But if a theory of race as a social invention simply reduces society to the operation of prejudices and restraints between groups and individuals, it can only add to the confusions in the current discourse. It ends up as a radical version of the upside-down view that racism is a subjective product of individuals, rather than the institutionalized creation of an elitist society.

To properly address racial division, we must locate it not in society in the abstract, but in the forms of organization and control prevalent in American society today. That is the road down which this study is attempting to take the debate.

2. THE POLITICS OF RACE

Race is now the unspoken issue behind countless public debates and controversies in the United States. In the world of politics, attitudes towards every question from presidential appointees to spending and policing priorities are now, quite literally, colored by racial considerations. The major legal battles of the 1990s have also all had an important, though usually implicit, racial component: one needs only to think of the Rodney King saga, the Mike Tyson rape trial and its mirror image, the Kennedy Smith case, or the courtroom and media circus surrounding O.J. Simpson. The cultural and art spheres, too, have had their share of race-related controversies, over everything from movies like "Malcom X" or "Falling Down," to Ice T's rap lyrics.

The paradox is, however, that race, the most potent issue in American society today, is almost never openly mentioned in national political debate. Those who occupy the places of power at the top of the political system simply do not talk about it themselves, and tend to frown upon those who do. Perhaps the most striking example of this attitude came during the 1992 presidential election campaign. A poll took place a few short months after the fury of the Black ghetto had erupted in Los Angeles, in response to the acquittal of the police officers who had been videotaped beating a Black motorist, Rodney King. Despite the proximity of the elections to the rioting, one study notes that, "Race and ethnic-group violence were not, nor did they become, part of the political dialogue during the 1992 presidential campaign. This silence can only be regarded as a form of elite denial."[1]

If the Washington political class is under the influence of a form of elite denial, the American electorate appears to have far less reticence when it comes to identifying and expressing an opinion on racial issues. "In many areas," the New York Times has noted, "voters are lining up along racial lines."[2] We have already noted the extent to which, in the 1994 congressional polls, White voters backed the Republicans and Black voters stayed with the Democrats. Nor was this an aberration. In 1992, when the tide was running strongly in the opposite direction, sweeping the Republicans out of the White House and the Democrats in, the racial line was still identifiable in voting patterns. Even as Bill Clinton scored a remarkable victory and millions deserted the Republican camp, George Bush still retained a narrow majority among Whites who voted.

The fact that a pattern of "elite denial" on the race issue coincides with clear expressions of popular prejudice has helped to create a misleading impression of where the political impetus behind racial tensions comes from. Today, there is an increasing tendency among politicians and commentators of different persuasions to seek to explain the rise of racial undertones and issues as a phenomenon driven from below, by American public opinion. According to this view, the key factor has been an intensification of racial fears and insecurities among ordinary White citizens, often in response to an escalation of Black crime and drug abuse, and to the belief that Blacks were being given preferential treatment by the authorities.

Listen to the tales liberal politicians tell of confronting reactionary voters, and it would be easy to conclude that the majority of the U.S. electorate are instinctive racists whose prejudice undermines the good intentions of the political elite. "I watch focus group tapes and I listen to my voters at the town meetings," said one Democrat from the House of Representatives a few months before the 1992 presidential election, "and it's the same thing over and over. They think Blacks have an unfair advantage in the job market. They think politicians are all crooks...I came here [more than a decade ago] to change the world, and now it just ain't there."[3]

Similarly, plaintive cries could be heard all over the country after the Democrats were given a heavy beating in the November 1994 congressional elections. Bill Press, chair of the California Democratic Party, ascribed his party's defeat to its failure to tailor its priorities and image sufficiently to match the prejudices of the largest section of the active electorate—the White male American. "We're seen as the party that cares about African-Americans," complained Press, "the party that cares about Latinos, the party that cares about gays, the party that cares about women—and don't give a damn about White males. We aren't saying anything to that base."[4]

These Democratic explanations of their party's problems sum up the accepted liberal wisdom about where the impulse towards the politicization of race comes from today. It is apparently the fault of ordinary White voters, the people who attend town meetings, have deluded themselves that Blacks get the best deal, and are stubbornly deaf to the compassionate appeals of decent politicians. Faced with such ignorance and bigotry, the message seems to be, what can a well-meaning congressman do?

The notion that the more reactionary shift in popular attitudes has been the driving force in bringing racial issues to new prominence in America has important consequences. It suggests that those in authority have acted only under pressure from public opinion, that the government, the courts, the police, employers, the media, and others in positions of influence, have somehow felt obligated to take a firmer line on race-related issues in response to this popular pressure. This approach creates a from-the-bottom-upwards theory that explains where the new climate of racial tensions has come from the grassroots. It may be persuasively supported by opinion polls and attitude surveys, but it is in serious danger of turning reality on its head.

The reality is that the most important initiatives that have turned race into the number one issue in the United States today have come largely from the top of society downwards. This new focus has not been a case of a spontaneous outburst of racial panic or segregationist fervor among ordinary White Americans. Instead, the dominant elites in American society have effectively inflated, exploited, and manipulated questions of race and racial antagonism for their own sectional benefit. These elites have institutionalized racial divisions in this country. The responses of White Americans to the social and economic problems of the post-war period have been shaped by a ruling political culture in which racially charged issues have been given a central role.

The judiciary, the chiefs of police, the media barons, major employers, academics, and other pillars of American society have all played a part in institutionalizing the politics of race. Here we shall focus first on those elite forces which have combined to affect most greatly the shaping of the racial map of postwar America—that is, the Washington establishment, made up of the federal agencies and the ruling political class, which, for the purposes of this study, should be understood as encompassing the leading members of both major American parties. Together, the actions of both the Republican and Democratic parties over the past half-century, and particularly the past 25 years, have ensured that race exerts a silent but powerful influence on the American political and social agenda.

The recent history of race and U.S. politics demonstrates how the creation and exacerbation of racial tensions today has had little to do with the distant past of slavery, or with any inherent racism among White Americans, or with any "natural" response to a Black crime epidemic. Instead, the current situation has been largely brought about by the way in which the U.S. authorities have institutionalized an elitist, divisive political culture, which has acted to focus public concerns away from any critical examination of American society and onto more racially loaded issues, such as crime, taxation, and "the decline of American values."

The net result of this pattern of elite manipulation has been to instill White America with a heightened sense of race—effectively giving the green light to every redneck and bigot who wants to abuse Black people in public, to take a baseball bat to a Black youth in Bensonhurst, or to acquit police filmed beating a Black man in Los Angeles. Less publicly but even more importantly, the heightened consciousness of racial divisions brought about by elite intervention, has been a strong determining influence on the outlooks and attitudes of ordinary White citizens towards everyday issues.

UNDERSTANDING THE ISSUE

In coming to grips with the role of racial politics over recent decades, we need to examine the key area of the interaction between the political elites and the process of mass suburbanization that is sometimes called the "White flight" from the cities. This mass migration by Whites, coupled with the intensified ghettoization of the Black communities in the cities, has created the modern form of informal segregation in U.S. society. This spatial divide between Black and White America has been powerfully politicized around racially interpreted issues.

To grasp the implications of this process fully, we will find it useful to outline its development from the Second World War to the 1990s; to look at how the Republican Party used race as the "wedge" with which it broke the old Democratic Party coalition, attracted new suburban voters, and established GOP hegemony in the White House; and to examine how, in its subsequent efforts to turn the electoral tide once more and win over White middle-class voters, the Democratic Party has made crucial concessions to the conservative viewpoint in every race-related debate.

Before we survey this history, however, it is worthwhile trying to establish a basic understanding of the relationship that has formed between elitist politics and the mass of White suburbanites around the issue of race. It is a relationship between two factors: on the one hand, the aspirations and insecurities of White Americans, which need not necessarily have any connection with racial matters; and on the other hand, the divisive and discriminatory political culture, institutionalized from the top down, which has often caused those aspirations and insecurities to be reinterpreted through the prism of race prejudice and antagonism towards the Black urban "underclass."

The major motivation behind the "White flight" to the suburbs was not any subjective wish to create racially "pure" enclaves. It should be obvious that, in and of itself, there is nothing racist about moving out of the city to leafier districts. The major motivating factor in this migration was the wish among White Americans to obtain a better life for themselves and their families. And for most, that meant leaving the crumbling city centers.

Urban decay was not a natural or inevitable process. It was a consequence of the stagnation of the American economy, and of investment and planning decisions made by major employers and government bodies. As old industries closed, more businesses moved out of the cities when government failed to invest in the urban infrastructure; and the great population centers, which had grown up in the nineteenth and early twentieth centuries, fell into disrepair and disrepute. Moving out to find work and a better living environment became an increasingly attractive option for White Americans. It was also, of course, an attractive option for Black Americans; but as we shall see, for most of them that option was closed by a modern system of segregation.

The simple act of moving out to the suburbs need not necessarily have given rise to a new, more politicized consciousness of race. But the social environment and political climate in which the "White flight" took place ensured that it did. The way in which institutionalized segregation ensured that Blacks remained trapped in the ghetto heightened the sense among White suburbanites that moving up the social ladder meant leaving "them" behind. Blacks became more closely identified in the public mind with all the ills of urban blight—crime, poverty, drugs, bad housing—that people wanted to escape from. The aspiration to make a better life for your family turned into a wish to get further away from the brutalized districts where Blacks were concentrated. It was this sentiment, based upon the segregation of living space, that the elites had done much to institutionalize; they were then able to politicize it by connecting White insecurities to coded, racially divisive issues.

As we shall see, the Republican Party did the most to politicize race in the suburbs in the decades that followed the Second World War. But it did not do so by canvassing for support on an openly anti-Black platform. Such up-front racism had been discredited by the Nazi experience. And in any case, it could not appeal to the real concerns of White suburbanites, which were not about race as such, but about economic and social insecurity. What the political elite did instead was to mobilize around issues such as taxes, welfare, and crime, which touched upon the real fears among White voters while sending them a clear, if coded, racial message: that the Blacks of the inner cities, with their welfare demands, drug crime, and immorality were responsible for the problems facing Whites and their families.

The net result of this process has been to create a situation in which many ordinary Whites see poor Blacks as a threat to their social status. This is an outlook captured well by many attitude surveys and opinion polls, never more clearly than in a study of working-class White voters commissioned by the Michigan Democrats in 1985 to find out why the Democrats' "natural" constituency was now voting heavily Republican. It found that the White workers talked contemptuously about Blacks as, "the explanation for their vulnerability and for almost everything that has gone wrong in their lives; *not being Black is what constitutes being middle class; not living with Blacks is what makes a neighborhood a decent place to live*" (emphasis added).[5]

Accuse the subjects of these studies of harboring racist prejudices, and most will deny it absolutely. Of course, they insist, they have nothing against people with Black skin; it's just that those people down there live differently than we do. The extent to which racial tensions are often encoded within issues of culture and communal identity today was captured wonderfully in a profile of Simi Valley, the White suburb where police officers were originally acquitted of beating Rodney King, written by Jane Gross in the wake of the trial and subsequent Los Angeles riots. Gross interviewed several Simi Valley residents, all of whom emphasized that their suspicions were directed not against Black people as such but against those people who did not match their suburban image of decent Americans:

"Residents insist that what binds them is not their common race or ethnicity, but a shared middle-class lifestyle. 'We like living in a place with educated people, people who believe as we do,' said Brian Arkin, 'But I don't believe skin color is a criteria.'

'There's a Black person up our street and we say "Hi" like he's a normal person,' Mr. Arkin continued. 'This isn't about race. Its about whether you let your property run down.' 'Or whether you sell drugs out of your house,' his wife, Valerie, interjected."[6] Or, they might have added, whether you are on welfare, or an unmarried mother, or your kids blast rap music, or you display any of the other identifying stigmata of inner-city Blacks. And if you manage to avoid any of that deviant behavior, you can be treated "like you're a normal person." With normal, non-racial prejudices like that, who needs open racism?

Such outlooks among suburban Americans have been forged by the interaction between White flight, institutionalized segregation, and the manipulations of the political elites. These forces have turned the legitimate aspirations of working-class White Americans for a better life, and the insecurities bred by the failure of the American system to guarantee it, into a powerful sense of racial division. The development of that process is in many ways the story of modern American politics, as the following survey shows.

ETHNIC ORIGINS

The sea change of American politics during the second half of the twentieth century can perhaps best be described as a shift from the rule of the City to the rule of the Suburbs, a development paralleled in the sphere of ideas by the switch of emphasis from the politics of ethnicity to the politics of race. The change brought with it a transfer of federal power from the Democratic Party to the Republicans. The Democratic Party's subsequent campaign to get back into the White House has been based far less on genuinely challenging the new politics of race than on accommodating them—despite Democratic initiatives such as the civil rights legislation of the sixties or, in the nineties, Bill Clinton's emphasis upon encouraging "diversity."

For 20 years following Franklin Delano Roosevelt's election in 1932, the Democratic Party appeared to be the national party in the United States. After the Eisenhower years in the fifties, the Democrats returned to the White House during the Kennedy-Johnson era of 1960-68. It appeared that the Democratic alliance was best placed to hold the country together. But in fact, the old New Deal alliance had already been undermined by demographic changes and the political shifts that accompanied them.

In the age when the Democratic Party was on top, Democratic politics were premised upon relating to a constituency primarily through the language and images of nationalism and ethnicity, rather than nationalism and race. The modern American nation was created through waves of immigration of different ethnic groups in the late nineteenth and early twentieth centuries. Through this process, a unique national identity was formed. It typically combined a fierce sense of patriotism—the belief that the United States was the best Goddamn country in the world—with a pride in the ethnic origins of each immigrant group. It was a national identity most commonly expressed through the use of designations such as "Italian-American," "Irish-American," and so on.

The Democrats were to become the premier party of ethnicity. As the new immigrant working classes flooded into the northern cities, the partial integration of these immigrants was overseen by the big Democratic machines in city hall. Through a combination of patronage and appeals to ethnic-American patriotism, the Democratic Party established its leading influence within the immigrant groups. Having partially succeeded in associating the Republicans with the rich old WASP elite in the public mind, the Democrats promoted themselves as the party of the people(s), of the aspirant immigrant working men and women. Typically, on July 4, 1915, Woodrow Wilson's Democratic administration staged Americanization Day under the slogan "Many Peoples, One Nation."

It is not difficult to question whether the Democratic Party leadership adopted such pluralistic slogans and principles out of a heartfelt belief in the equality of ethnic and racial groups. Indeed, the Democrats seemed prepared to turn against ethnic identities if they appeared likely to interfere with the pursuit of the strategic interests of the WASP elite; for example, in 1916 Wilson branded as "hyphenated Americans" those who pressed him to support Ireland's right to national self-determination.

Nevertheless, appealing to the politics of ethnicity served the Democratic Party well enough. The Democrats managed to negotiate the competing claims of ethnically defined sections of society on the basis of an expanding economy. The European immigration at the turn of the century, largely consisting of Italians and Jews, was the last population shift to move into a rapidly expanding American economy. Each group, it appeared, could take their turn at the bottom of the ladder of opportunity, only to move up a rung with the next wave of immigration. Ethnic identification proved to be a compensation for discrimination and a launching pad for success. Within the cities, the ethnic communities provided protection and encouraged a spirit of self-help amongst its members. It was largely on the basis of forging a relationship with these new immigrant, working-class communities in the North that the Democratic Party established its national leadership.

A major report delivered to Congress in 1910 revealed that in major cities such as New York and Chicago, two out of every three children were the sons and daughters of immigrants. In 1932, the influence of the Democratic Party machines ensured that the children of that generation of urban immigrants played a key part in electing F.D.R., backing his New Deal, and apparently establishing the Democrats as the part of modern America.

The Democratic Party's success was founded upon the alliance between southern conservatives and northern minorities and Blacks. The weak link built into the chain was the issue of race. This was to prove a major weapon in the Republicans' attempt to break that Democratic alliance apart.

Under Roosevelt, the Democrats embarked upon new initiatives to win Black support in both the North and the South. Eleanor Roosevelt fronted much of this initial campaigning, setting up a "Black cabinet" to advise on urban policy. Much of this looks like the politics of gesture and tokenism. For example, despite all of the administration's promises of equality, as the war economy got going Black workers continued to suffer discrimination; only 4.5 percent of Fair Employment Practices Committee placements in 20 defense industries had gone to Blacks in 1940, falling to 2.5 percent in 1941. Nevertheless, Roosevelt's Democrats were winning a reputation as the party that was concerned more about race.

The Democratic leadership's initiatives infuriated the old racist "Dixiecrats" down south, who had long kept Blacks out of the party and under their thumb. Southern conservatives, finding their party hijacked by outsiders who seemed bent on undermining racial segregation, rebelled. Feeling their power and influence under threat from the wide-ranging social changes implemented under the New Deal era, the "Dixiecrats" focused their fears and insecurities on the threat of the "uppity nigger," which they now associated with Roosevelt's party. In the 1942 elections, some southern conservatives stood against official Democratic candidates. For example, Eugene Talmadge stood in Georgia, saying "We love the Negro in his place, but his place is at the back door."[7]

The southern conservatives were a minority, but their influence was growing through the forties. The importance of racial tensions in America was brought home with dramatic impact by the Detroit race riots of 1943, in which 43 people died. With hindsight, it is possible to say that the writing was on the wall for the Democratic alliance when conservative southern delegates walked out of the party convention in 1948; the Dixiecrats split after a platform position was read out which declared that "The Democratic Party commits itself to continuing its efforts to eradicate all racial, religious and economic discrimination." Truman's Democrats survived that split to win the 1948 presidential election, against the expectations of most. But it had been demonstrated that race was an issue that could split the Democratic coalition asunder. That situation was to be exploited by the Republican Right to create a new constituency in the post-war era. The politics of race would finally and fully come into their own from the late sixties, with the vital assistance of developments in society supervised by government agencies and major employers.

THE "WHITE FLIGHT"

The shift from the politics of ethnicity to the politics of race in the postwar era can in part be seen as the political dimension of a movement of power and influence from the cities to the suburbs. The population exodus from the old urban centers, the "White flight," as it has sometimes been called, helped to create the raw demographic material for the new racial culture, by erecting a more stark physical division between the worlds of White and Black America. But that is not to suggest that the process of moving to the suburbs was itself somehow sufficient to make White Americans think in more directly racial terms.

The racially exclusive fashion in which suburbanization took place was a process largely controlled by government agencies and major corporations. Political elites then exploited the new situation so as to harden the city-suburb divide into a political split along mainly racial lines.

The "White flight" to the suburbs was not a natural movement, like the migration of birds. It was strictly regimented under the control of U.S. government agencies. As Douglas Massey and Nancy Denton have noted in their excellent study of these developments, "the distinguishing feature of racial segregation in the post-war era is the direct role that government played not only in maintaining the color line but in strengthening the walls of the ghetto."[8] The segregation of suburbia was the consequence, not merely of grassroots prejudice, but of decisions made at the highest levels of American society to encourage and systematize an effective apartheid pattern of housing.

To listen to some conservatives talk today about the need for unemployed urban Blacks to "move to where the jobs are," you would think that Black people had remained in the inner-city ghettos out of choice, that they had turned down the opportunity to move to the suburbs. The truth is that from the time large-scale suburbanization began in the 1920s, it was organized along racially exclusive lines in order to create all-White residential strongholds —with the full support of the U.S. government agencies.

The suburban segregationist policy, which was adopted in the first place by the realtors and mortgage companies, was known as "red-lining." Mortgage companies simply refused to lend on properties that were considered to be at risk of losing value because of the prospect of Blacks moving into an area. Maintaining property values thus gave a "reasonable" rationale to an exclusive racial solidarity. The property buyers' two bibles—*Babcock's Valuation of Real Estate* (1932) and *McMichael's Appraising Manual* (1931)—both indicated that the presence of "undesirable elements" was sufficient grounds to refuse a loan. This policy was not only an effective sanction against prospective Black buyers, but was also a good way to put pressure on White homeowners to help keep Blacks out and so protect the value of their property.

In the thirties, racially motivated "red-lining" effectively became federal government policy. As the Depression struck America, the Roosevelt administration stepped in to provide cheap housing loans, both to boost the construction industry and to offset possible suburban unrest over foreclosures. It set up the Home Owners Loan Corporation (HOLC)—but only a certain type of homeowner needed apply. The HOLC brought on board the racial component of suburban housing policy, and red-lining became institutionalized.

The HOLC instituted a system of grading for neighborhood factors, upon which the decision to grant mortgages was based. "A" areas were in demand in good times and bad, and were homogeneous, meaning "American business or professional men." "B" areas were "still desirable," "C" were "declining," while "D" had declined. Black areas were invariably put in "D," while those areas "within such a low price or rent range as to attract undesirable elements" were put in "C." These grades were systematically applied to secret HOLC maps of all metropolitan ares, dividing each neighborhood up according to its existing, and predicted, racial character.[9]

The major impact of the HOLC was in setting standards that were adopted by the other two federal agencies that were to have a more profound impact on the patterns of suburbanization in the forties and fifties—the Federal Housing Administration (FHA) and the Veterans Administration (VA). The millions of dollars of relatively cheap loans pumped into the housing market by these bodies was a major stimulus to rapid suburbanization after 1945, as more and more Americans bought their own homes. The FHA financed the suburbs on the basis of the HOLC's race maps and its segregationist ethos.

The FHA's *Underwriting Manual* (1939) emphasized the importance of keeping out "inharmonious racially or nationality groups" and recommended the use of "subdivisions, regulations, and suitably restrictive covenants" to achieve their exclusion. These covenants, forbidding a buyer to sell to a Negro, were a common condition of sale. The FHA's use of detailed maps of racial mix provided a powerful incentive to segregation. "In a March 1939 map of Brooklyn, for example, the presence of a single, non-White family on any block was sufficient to make that entire block Black"—and thereby exclude all the occupants from assistance with mortgages.[10]

So it was the developers and the government that created the all-White suburbs on the outskirts of many American cities. The "Jim Crow" covenants kept Blacks out of the growing suburbs both before and after the Second World War. By the early 1950s, one perceptive liberal commentator already understood the racial element of suburbanization—and the responsibility of federal agencies for shaping the suburbs in such a segregated way:

"A government offering such bounty to builders and lenders could have required compliance with a non-discrimination policy. Instead FHA adopted a racial policy that could well have been culled from the Nueremberg Laws. From its inception FHA set itself up as the protector of the all-White neighborhood. It sent its agents into the field to keep Negroes and other minorities from buying homes in White neighborhoods."[11]

Seen from this perspective, suburbanization—the "White flight"—clearly trapped many Blacks, and later Latinos, in the inner-city ghettos, whether they liked it or not.

Unlike the immigration of the late nineteenth and early twentieth centuries, the next great demographic shift in America was internal: the northern migration of impoverished Black sharecroppers in the period from 1930 to 1960. Blacks had already been recruited to fill northern jobs left by Whites during World War I, only to be driven out of the cities in peace time. When the process was repeated during World War II, and southern agriculture collapsed, the dislocation of southern Blacks was complete. Between 1930 and 1960, three million Blacks moved northwards to the industrial cities.

The Blacks who came north were moving into the margins of heavy industry, to be used as a reserve army of labor or as tools to break trade unions, as Henry Ford did in securing a non-unionized Black workforce. Black migration north did not fit the past pattern of a new ethnic group integrating into an expanding economy. Instead, as Blacks moved into the already-declining inner cities, Whites moved out to the suburbs.

Meanwhile, the Black ghettos themselves were being hemmed in all the more tightly by the government policies of urban renewal and public-housing construction. The clearing of slums and building of housing projects was carried out in such a way that the area of the city in which poor Blacks could live became increasingly confined and isolated. Massey and Denton describe the public-housing projects that had been built in America's large cities by the 1970s as "Black reservations, highly segregated from the rest of society and characterized by extreme social isolation."[12] For Arnold Hirsch, public housing has become an officially sanctioned "second ghetto...solidly institutionalized and frozen in concrete," where "government took an active hand not merely in reinforcing prevailing patterns of segregation, but in lending them a permanence never seen before."[13]

The accelerating process of postwar suburbanization, and the impact it was to have, were greatly aided by the attitude of employers. The corporate elite of America—first in modern industries like defense, aerospace and technology, and then in the service-sector companies of the 1980s boom—moved their plants and back offices away from the city centers, and invested heavily in the burgeoning White suburbs. As a consequence, employment patterns became increasingly set along racial lines, with most Blacks being shut out of professional, executive, and skilled jobs just as effectively as they were shut out of the better residential areas.

This trend continued with varying degrees of intensity throughout the postwar decades. By the end of the 1980s' economic boom, reporter Mike Davis was able to make a withering observation about the role that corporate America's policy of investing in the White suburban counties around Los Angeles and ignoring the city itself had played in increasing the segregation of the labor market. While the suburbs had enjoyed an extended service-sector boom in the Reagan years, Davis noted that areas like South Central just kept on getting poorer.

"It is a stunning fact—emblematic of institutionalized racism on a far more rampant scale than usually admitted these days—that most of California's 1980s job and residential growth areas—southern Orange County, eastern Ventura County, northern San Diego County, Contra Costa County, and so on—have Black populations of ONE PERCENT OR LESS."[14]

Despite considerable economic growth in the region in the late eighties, the rate of unemployment among Black youth in Los Angeles did not move; it remained at an awesome 45 percent.

Postwar suburbanization had a profound impact on the shape of American politics. In his seminal work *The Emerging Republican Majority*, Kevin Phillips described the changes in the New York area:

"The 1952 election confirmed the tentative beginning of a new era in North-Eastern politics—the rise of suburbia. In the wake of World War II and the increased prosperity which it had engendered, many urban North Easterners looked around for new housing in the suburbs. At first only the affluent were able to move, but by mid-century, a great middle-class trek was also under way. This trend caused the big city impetus to lose headway. For fifty years, the percentage of the New York State vote cast by New York City residents had been rising. In 1944…it had reached 52 percent; now that percentage began to decline as suburban power fattened on the exodus from the central cities."[15]

This was the beginning of a process through which the suburbs would replace the cities as the centers of electoral influence in the United States—culminating in the 1992 election, when suburban America finally exercised a majority of the nation's votes. The way in which those suburban voters approach issues has been crucially influenced by the racial culture that political and cultural elites have constructed. This culture has been built on the foundations that were laid and reinforced by the formal and informal segregationist policies, both of government bodies like the Federal Housing Authority and of the major U.S. corporations.

THE POLITICS OF RACE

For those moving out to the suburbs in the decades after World War II, or only aspiring to do so, the new circumstances created the potential for a new cultural and political identification. This potential was to be exploited by the Republican Party to forge a new suburban political identity.'

The process of suburbanization broke up the traditional White ethnic enclaves of the cities. Removed from the geographic and cultural contexts of the old neighborhoods, third and fourth generation immigrants no longer identified themselves principally as members of an ethnic-American grouping. They became instead subsumed into membership of the great White American middle class. Because ethnic tensions and relations had been so central to city life, it was widely assumed that they would be reproduced in the suburbs. But they were not. One sociologist who went into the suburbs expecting to find new ethnic enclaves found instead that there was no significant ethnic dimension to suburban politics. Rather, "the racial problem had most electoral impact."[16]

The issue of racial segregation in the suburbs and its political implications was not seriously aired in public debate until after the 1960s' explosions of Black anger in the cities highlighted the divide in dramatic fashion. The National Advisory Council on Civil Disorder, chaired by Otto Kerner, was sent to find out what was behind the urban revolts. Its report outlined the process by which White America largely left Black America behind in the ghetto.

"The later phase of Negro settlement and expansion in metropolitan areas diverges sharply from those typical of White immigrants. As the Whites were absorbed by larger society, many left their predominantly ethnic neighborhoods and moved to outlying areas to obtain newer housing and better schools. Some scattered randomly over the suburban area. Others established new ethnic clusters in the suburbs, but even these rarely constituted solely members of a single ethnic group. As a result, most middle class neighborhoods —both in the suburbs and within the central cities—have no distinctive ethnic character, EXCEPT THAT THEY ARE WHITE."[17]

The dislocation of suburbanization created a situation where, for millions of White Americans, their identity was no longer part of an ethnic cultural plurality but part of a racial divide. Moving also broke the links with the city-based Democratic machines. The Republicans had the opportunity to garner new votes, and they did so by focusing politics around racially loaded issues and themes.

It is important to stress once again here that we are discussing a process of manipulation and exploitation of the racial issue by the elites. White working people did not leave the cities in order to form a racist bloc. In many ways, moving to the suburbs is a rational response to inner-city deprivation. But suburbanization has taken place within a social environment and political climate that have ensured that this moment took on racial overtones. With economic and political discrimination ensuring that Blacks were concentrated in ghettos, it was not difficult to attach racial implications to the mass movement of White people away from those areas. Black neighborhoods were associated with deprivation and crime in the public imagination. For most Whites, self-improvement became closely linked with putting distance between their family and the places where Black people lived.

In effect, Blacks had moved from a state of formal segregation in the South to an informal segregation in the North. It was only a short step from there for the politicians, ably assisted by the forces of law and order and by the media, to create a siege mentality among suburban Whites. The message was this: having moved away from "those districts," we must protect what we've got—our homes, jobs, property values, and serenity— from the incursions of "those people," whether those incursions take the form of crime or demands for more public spending to subsidize the cities. White suburbia was put on guard to support the police, hire security guards, and refuse to pay more tax dollars.

When the Democratic administrations of the early sixties passed civil rights legislation, Republican politicians responded by trying to prey on White insecurities that Blacks' demands were being pandered to—a message that had more impact after the inner-city riots of the mid-sixties. White Americans became more open to the suggestion that they should organize to protect what they had from others—and in the first place, that meant against the impoverished Blacks from the inner cities. This idea was cultivated by politicians, quite subtly on the national stage, but crudely at the local level.

REPUBLICAN WEDGE

The new racial politics favored the Republican Party. It became a weapon to break up the Democratic coalition. As the Edsalls have argued, race was in many ways the perfect "wedge issue" that the Republicans could drive into the traditional liberal coalition, by inflating and preying on White fears about alleged preferential hiring of Blacks or the supposed prospect of higher taxes to pay for group-specific social programs.[18]

Richard Nixon appealed to these concerns in the 1968 presidential election, when he defeated the Democratic Party candidate Hubert Humphrey. The Democrats were already feeling the impact of the politics of race. The civil rights reforms and War on Poverty pursued by the Kennedy and Johnson administrations in the early sixties had some success in integrating a layer of middle-class Blacks into the Democratic cause. (Whether the mass of ordinary Black people still living in degrading poverty were inspired by the apparent effort towards equality of a civil rights bill is open to question.) But these programs also offered ammunition to the Republicans in their attempt to get White voters to identify themselves in opposition to the Black inner cities.

George Wallace's segregationist candidacy in 1968 won five southern states and 13.6 percent of the national vote, stealing White support away from the Democrats and providing a stepping-stone to White voters' switch to the Republicans. Nixon himself was too cautious to play the race card so openly. Instead, he used the sort of coded language or doublespeak that has since come to dominate political discussions. He alluded to the "divisiveness" of the Democrats' civil rights policies. Nixon talked about law and order in ways that associated the Democratic Party with the inner cities and Black crime. By giving political shape and leadership to a White identity emerging in the suburbs, the Republicans took votes from the Democrats all over the country.

Kevin Phillips, an advisor to campaign manager John Mitchell in the 1968 campaign, believes that the Nixon election marked a fundamental shift in U.S. politics. In *The Emerging Republican Majority*, Phillips gives useful insights into Republicans' reading of the race issue. Phillips advised President Nixon to plan ahead for victory in 1972 by making a home for all those Democrats attracted by the segregationist Wallace. "Negro-Democratic mutual identification," he wrote, "was a major source of Democratic loss." The Republicans' best bet now was to play on (and play up) White resentment about "Negro demands." By encouraging a clear racial divide and aligning itself firmly with the White side, Phillips suggested, "the GOP can build a winning coalition without Negro votes."[19]

In an interview published two years into that first Nixon administration, Phillips spelt out the Republican aim of encouraging an exclusive, White-suburban identity. "We don't need the big cities," he announced, "don't even want them." What they wanted instead, it seemed, were enemies against whom they could unite their constituency." The whole secret of politics," said Phillips, "is knowing who hates you."[20] Or, he might have said, knowing whom it will pay you to hate.

Perhaps the politics of race came into their own most explicitly 20 years later, in the Republican strategy pursued around the presidential election campaign of 1988. Ronald Reagan had served his two terms and failed to deliver on his promise to the American people of prosperity and pride. There were fears—supported by early polls—that perhaps the Democrats might make a comeback under the candidacy of Michael Dukakis. The politics of race changed all of that, primarily in the person of Willie Horton.

Horton, a convicted first-degree murderer ineligible for parole in Massachusetts, was given a weekend furlough, during which he tortured a man and raped his fiancee. The Bush campaign highlighted the case in television advertisements, designed to demonstrate that furlough-supporting Democrats like Dukakis were on the side of the dangerous minority against the decent majority of American citizens. The Willie Horton advertisements were only the front line of a Republican campaign intended to prey on the economic and social insecurities of White Americans and turn them against the alleged unholy alliance of Blacks and Democratic liberals.

The issue of quotas, which had been on the table for 20 years, also figured prominently in the Bush campaign. It was a device used to address White fears about unemployment in such a way as to suggest that Blacks, cosseted by liberals, were responsible for Whites losing their jobs. Through this breathtaking racist trick, the Republicans were able to turn the mass unemployment that they had presided over into an argument for voting Republican! Two years later, Senator Jesse Helms was to win North Carolina against the odds with an anti-quotas campaign focused on images of Black hands taking from White hands.

After the 1988 presidential election victory, Representative Newt Gingrich of Georgia, then the House Republican whip, boasted to the *Washington Post* of the success of his party's campaign to polarize public opinion in this way. "Now," said Gingrich, "we have a way of dividing America." He was referring to what he calls "value-laden" issues: crime, drugs, education, etc. He did not need to spell out that he was really describing the politics of race, presented in the coded form which has matured through the postwar era in America, and which political elites have used to polarize opinion and politicize the racial divide from the top down.[21]

RACE IN THE NINETIES

The 1990s have seen the opening up of another chapter in the politics of race in the United States. In the first major political contest of the decade, the presidential election of 1992, the announcement of a "cultural war" against the Black communities of the inner cities failed to win the White House for the Republicans in the way that the race card had in 1988. It was tempting to suggest, as some prominent commentators did in the aftermath of Bill Clinton's election, that the racially charged climate of the Reagan-Bush years was finished. But things proved not to be so straightforward. The key factor has been the concessions that Clinton Democrats made, both during and after the campaign, to the agenda that the Republicans had established over the previous decades.

As a section of the political elite, the Democratic Party has become an integral part of the post-liberal consensus on the relationship between the Black poor and U.S. society. Far from challenging the Republican view on questions such as crime, welfare, and the "underclass," the Democrats have adapted these issues for their own purposes. As a consequence, the hostile policies of the Reagan-Bush years on these issues continued to be reinforced from the top down, despite the change of personalities in Washington. In the short term, this adaptation by the Democratic Party elite was to create the conditions in which the Republicans could make a comeback, in the 1994 congressional elections, around the issues of taxes and crime. In the longer term, we are left with a situation where it appears that so long as the reins of power are simply passed back and forth between the elites of the Republicans and Democrats, racial issues will remain a potent political force for conservatism in American society.

To make things clearer, let us review the role of race in the 1992 presidential election campaign. This review should help us to come to terms with the way in which the Republicans and the Democrats, far from representing genuinely opposed viewpoints, act as different sections of the same political class, which has institutionalized racial thinking. As such, their election campaigns can be seen as popularizing the same kind of elitist notions in slightly different languages.

Desperate to reclaim support they had lost during a deep economic recession, the Republican Right attempted to go for broke during the 1992 campaign. At the Republican Party convention, one of the key opening addresses was delivered by Pat Buchanan, the "paleo-conservative." He sought to set the tone for a frenzied last lap of campaigning by announcing the "cultural war":

"There is a religious war going on in this country for the soul of America. It is a cultural war, as critical to the kind of nation we shall be as the Cold War itself, for this war is for the soul of America. And in that struggle for the soul of America, Clinton and Clinton [Bill and Hillary] are on the other side, and George Bush is on our side."[22]

Buchanan's moral battle lines were clear, as were the implications for race-related issues. George Bush was on "our side," the side of Middle America, with its decent, suburban values. Clinton's Democrats were on "the other side," along with rioters, welfare queens, crack-dealers, pornographers, and pimps. Just to drive home the point, Buchanan ended his call to arms with an analogy based upon images of the Los Angeles riots. Just as the courageous young troops of the 18th Cavalry had fought to retake the streets of that city, block by block, so he told the assembled delegates, "we must take back OUR cities, and take back OUR culture and take back OUR country."[23]

Buchanan's speech reworked the themes of an earlier address that he delivered to Jerry Falwell's Liberty College soon after the Los Angeles riots in May. Then, the racial content of the cultural war had been spelt out in even more militaristic fashion:

"Friends, make no mistake; what we saw in Los Angeles was evil exultant and triumphant, and we no longer saw it as through a glass darkly, but face to face...And you do no deal with the Vandals and Visigoths who are pillaging your cities by expanding the Head Start and food stamp programs."[24]

This was the politicization of race taken to new heights of hysteria. As part of his general reassertion of reactionary values, Buchanan brought together and intensified all of the diverse elements of the Right's propaganda offensive against the Black urban "underclass"—crime, violence, welfare payments, etc.— to label his enemies as "barbarians" and launch a "cultural war" against them. Buchanan's use of religious imagery and language did little to disguise the fact that his was essentially a race war. After all, surveys purport to show that Blacks in the United States are among the most ardent Christians on Earth, which did not prevent Buchanan from branding the Black communities of the American inner city as "the barbarian...inside the gates."

The explanation for Buchanan's outburst lies in his suggestion that the cultural war was as crucial as the Cold War had been. The end of the Cold War and the collapse of the Soviet Union have closed an era in U.S. politics. This collapse gave the Republicans the opportunity for some short-term triumphalism about defeating communism. But it soon became clear that the removal of the "Red Menace" had also robbed the U.S. Right of the central plank of its postwar worldview. New problems of incoherence and a lack of focus became apparent among Republicans. This loss of direction took on particular importance against the background of deepening economic recession and societal crisis.

With the external focus of the Soviet enemy gone, America looked in on itself, and many did not like what they saw. The Republican coalition fractured under the pressures created by the end of the Cold War and the start of a major economic slump. Buchanan's challenge to Bush for the nomination and the sudden rise of Ross Perot were both reflections of the dissatisfaction felt within the essentially suburbanite constituency that the Republicans have held together over the past 25 years. The so-called White, middle-class silent majority is no longer so silent, or so impressed by attempts to display U.S. power abroad when things are falling apart at home. "Saddam Hussein's still got his job, have you got yours?" read the 1992 bumper sticker in New Hampshire.

The Right's lack of a "vision thing" with which to inspire renewed support threatened to do serious damage to the Republican base in the post-Cold War era. The launch of a cultural war at the party convention was an attempt to compensate for this shortcoming. It demonstrated the willingness of a conservative clique to resort to barely-coded declarations of race hatred in a bid to rally their fragmenting forces and garner support. But this strategy was only an extreme example of the established practice of the U.S. political elite—seeking to manipulate the fears and insecurities of White voters by focusing on racially loaded issues. Teetering on the edge of defeat, the Republican Right resorted to the classic divide-and-conquer tactics of war.

The rantings of Buchanan failed to exert any powerful influence over the political agenda in the 1992 election. Without the broader ideological framework of "good vs. evil" that had been provided for the Republicans by the old Cold War polarities and against the background of deep recession and economic failure under Bush, such a direct and divisive appeal from the far right had little chance of success. Indeed, the Republicans proved incapable even of pressing the case for their cultural war outside the convention hall; Buchanan's hardline messages about driving out the barbarians never really featured in George Bush's campaign for re-election.

Thus Bush, in 1992, was unable to recreate the Willie Horton effect of 1988. But nobody should be under any illusions. The election results did not mean the end of the elite's attempts to politicize the racial divide and direct public discontent against the Black "underclass." The key factor here, which we will now turn to consider, was the adaptation of the Democratic Party elite to the Republican agenda, and the extent to which the Democrats took their place in the post-liberal consensus that has come to dominate the discussion of social policy today.

THE DEMOCRATS: "WE GOT 'EM UNDER CONTROL"

Bill Clinton's election to the White House created many false hopes and illusions among liberal-minded observers. Almost on the eve of polling in the 1992 presidential race, a leading commentator noted what he saw as a major change of mood in American politics:

"In every presidential election since 1968, the middle-class concerns of race and crime have been at the center of campaign debate. This year, they have scarcely been discussed.[25]

Well, yes and no. It may well have been the case that there were no Willie Horton advertising campaigns this time around and that the Republican Right's more hysterical rhetoric about race and crime failed to connect sufficiently to cause a meaningful discussion. But the more significant point is surely that the encoded, race-related issues are now so firmly embedded in the foundations of American politics that they do not need to be raised explicitly in order to exert an influence. If the prejudices bred by institutionalized discrimination are not directly challenged, they will continue to hold sway over American society regardless of the content of election campaign advertisements.

In this respect, what Bill Clinton's campaign didn't say was just as significant as what it did say. In failing to make a serious attempt to challenge the underlying assumptions of the elitist approach to the Black communities of the inner cities, the Democrats pandered to these assumptions. In so doing, they ensured that although the Republican majority fractured, the racial politics upon which it was built have continued to cast a lengthening shadow over American society.

It is rather ironic that the hard-pressed Republicans should have sought to generate support by labeling Clinton a "leftist" friend of welfare recipients and rioters, or by trying to brand the Democratic Party as what radio talk-show host Rush Limbaugh calls "Commie-libs." Nothing could be further from the truth than the idea that the Democrats of the 1990s are fifth columnists for communism in the United States.

On many of the fundamental issues, the modern Democratic Party does not represent a genuine political alternative to the Republicans. Instead, the Democratic Party leadership can be seen as a competing section of the same elite political class. As such, its primary concern is with acquiring and maintaining power and control —not with achieving radical change or social justice. The ambitions of the Democratic elite are closely bound up with maintaining the same powerful institutions of American society that the Republicans rely upon. The Democrats may be prepared to see a change in the race and gender of some of those at the top of these government institutions. But they have neither the interest nor the will to challenge the institutionalized discrimination and top-down divisions that marginalize the majority of America's Black communities.

The Democratic Party's strategy for regaining presidential office in the 1992 election was framed within the established parameters of elite politics. Clinton's campaign sought to highlight the issue that was causing most concern among Republican voters—the failures of economic management that were seen to be responsible for the recession of the later Bush years. At the same time that they emphasized these economic questions, however, the Democrats sought to avoid any political controversy that might alienate them from their target audience—suburbanite Republican voters. Instead, they remolded their program to accommodate the prejudices instilled by the top-down politicization of race over the previous two decades. As a consequence, their "alternative" to the Right's cultural war turned out to be a coded repackaging of familiar Republican prejudices—on public spending, on welfare and, by implication, on race. Far from challenging the conservative viewpoints, the Democrats largely presented their own version of the same elitist double standards.

The Clinton campaign carefully crafted its image to evoke similarities with the traditional Democratic Party—using the catchphrase "New Covenant," the picture of the young Clinton shaking hands with JFK, etc. In substance, however, the Democrats echoed themes more familiar to Republicans: their emphasis on "training" soon turned out to be a euphemism for workfare schemes; they criticized the so-called cycle of welfare dependency and demanded that fathers support their children;

they made no major public-spending promises and proposed only modest defense-spending cuts.

Leading Democratic Party figures demonstrated that they had studied well how to assume leadership of the Reaganite constituency by addressing it in the Black and White code. Writing in the *New Democrat*, Daniel Yankelovitch explained the implications of Clinton's tough New Covenant for taxation and welfare policies:

"If the society gives you a benefit, you must pay it back in some appropriate form. This means no more 'freebies,' no more rip-offs and no more unfairness to the middle class."[26]

Anybody familiar with the language of racial politics would immediately recognize the buzzwords in Yankelovitch's statement. Whatever he meant by them, the interpretation was clear enough. Those enjoying the "freebies" were obviously welfare recipients, which to many ears is just another way of saying "Black people" in American politics today. The "middle class" people suffering "unfairness," on the other hand, could only be the White suburbanites who complain about their tax dollars going to funding the ghetto lifestyle. In an inversion of reality that any conservative commentator would be proud of, Yankelovitch, the Democrat, turned the urban poor into the exploiters who are ripping off the suburbs.

On declaring his candidacy for the White House in Little Rock, Governor Clinton did announce his opposition to "race-baiting." Several times during his campaign, he also mentioned that he was opposed to those who preach "the politics of division." But as astute commentator Joan Didion pointed out, these apparently laudable statements were open to starkly conflicting interpretations.

From the point of view of the Democratic leadership, those who raised the problem of racism or spoke out for Black rights were the ones preaching the politics of division and race-baiting. Thus Clinton's team attacked his liberal rival, former California Governor Jerry Brown, for letting New York be "split apart by race," because Brown named Jesse Jackson as his preferred running mate. After the Los Angeles riots, Clinton himself gave a speech at Jackson's Rainbow summit, in which he railed against "hatred," "prejudice" and the practice of "pointing a finger at one another across racial lines." Ironically, however, the target of Clinton's attack was not the brutal racism of the LAPD or the media. It was Sister Soujah, a Black rapper and activist who had dared to suggest that the death of a White person during a riot would be no big deal to people in South Central Los Angeles, where Black people were dying violent deaths every day.

For the first time in close to 50 years, the 1992 Democratic Party program made no mention of redressing racial injustice. An expanded version of Bill Clinton's program, published in book form as *Putting People First,* barely refers to race at all. One chapter is called "Cities"; this title could be a problem for those seeking to appear conservative on racial issues, since "city" is itself now a virtual code word for "minorities." The chapter called "Program" resolved that difficulty, however, by failing to mention the term "inner city" or the realities of urban racial segregation. Another chapter is called "Civil Rights"; it says far more about the physically disabled, against whom few would run a hate campaign, than it does about the far more politically divisive question of Black rights. And when the book does mention race, it is in a promise to "oppose racial quotas"—a clear attempt to steal the Right's thunder on that racially charged issue.

On the eve of the Maryland, Georgia, and Colorado primaries, Clinton chose to have himself photographed in front of a formation of prisoners in chains, most of whom were Black, at the Stone Mountain Correctional Facility. Jerry Brown interpreted the imagery thus: "Two White men and 40 Black prisoners, what's he saying? He's saying 'We got 'em under control, don't worry.'"[27]

In one coded way or another, "We got 'em under control" is the message that politicians of all parties now seek to convey to their target constituency in Middle America. Having set up the Black urban "underclass" as a major problem facing suburban America, the different sections of the political elite now compete to prove that they are best equipped to police the bogeyman. The politicization of race, for so long the Republicans' most pointed weapon against the Democrats, has now become the basis of a cross-party consensus on key social-policy issues.

In an important sense, the 1992 U.S. Presidential election was an irrelevant circus. Whoever won, it made little substantial difference to the drift of race relations. Even if the outsider Ross Perot had miraculously triumphed, there would have been little chance of a change for the better from a man who proposed a military occupation of the inner cities—presumably to take "our" streets back, as Buchanan the cultural warrior would say.

Despite all of the ballyhoo about the dawning of a new era under Clinton, the presidential election confirmed that racial division and prejudice had been left intact by the Democrats' resurgence at the polls. The 38 percent of the popular vote won by George Bush was strongly based upon the support of White Middle America. And while enough "Reagan Democrats" returned to the Democratic fold to give Clinton 43 percent of the popular vote, that number cannot in any way be said to represent a real rejection of racial consciousness. Although these White voters were clearly unimpressed by the high-pitched screaming of the Republicans' "cultural war" during a devastating economic recession, their decision to vote for Clinton was not based on liberalism. Instead, it partly reflected a feeling that the new-look conservative Democrats were less likely than the old ones to make concessions to Black needs. For their part, Blacks voted overwhelmingly for Clinton; yet more Blacks than usual stayed at home, perhaps because they felt that they were being taken for granted by the Democrats.

Since the 1992 presidential election, the consequences of
the cross-party, post-liberal consensus within the elite have
become clear enough. The racial consciousness instilled from
the top down has remained intact despite—and partly because
of—Clinton's campaign and election. Thus, a couple of years
later, when the insecurities of White voters were turned once
again against the Democratic administration, the issues connected with race in the public mind gave the Republicans their
political focus. So questions like crime and taxes, which some
commentators claimed had lost their edge during the 1992
election campaign, came center-stage again. As the *New York
Times* noted, one of the reasons why so many men voted Republican in the November 1994 congressional elections was that
they had "become more sympathetic to hardline Republican
positions on issues like crime and taxes, which were central in
political campaigns this year."[28] Newt Gingrich's "contract"
with the middle classes aimed to put those positions into
practice after the elections.

The response of the Clinton administration to this setback
was equally telling. It sought to emphasize its commitment to
cutting back on welfare spending and cracking down on
crime—in other words, to waging a social-policy war of its own
against the "underclass" communities of the Black ghettos. The
convergence between different sections of the political elite
around an agenda of enforcing the racial divide in American
society can never have been clearer.

Nobody should be in any doubt as to the position of
racially loaded issues at the core of the post-liberal consensus
on social policy in the United States today. Those who ignore
the specific impact of race are in danger of missing the central
issue of our times. Thus one 1992 study of opinion polls sought
to demonstrate how the attitudes of the American public had
become more liberal over the previous, Republican-dominated
decade. While in general the poll data used by James A. Stimson did suggest something of a broad liberalization of attitudes

towards public spending among American voters, it significantly pointed in the opposite direction on certain specific issues. The most telling examples of this phenomenon came when people were asked the following three questions: were they willing to help Blacks; were they willing to help the poor; and did they favor harsher policies on matters of criminal justice. In these three cases, most voters had become more conservative, not more liberal. And given the close association of the issues of poverty and crime with race in the public consciousness, the implications of these results for gauging prevalent attitudes towards racial matters ought to be clear enough.[29]

The majority view in White America today holds Black America responsible for major social problems. This view is the pay-off for the hard work that the political elites have done in connecting insecurities to racial issues and diverting attention away from the failures of their economic and political system onto the supposed shortcomings of those at the bottom of society.

3. BLAMING BLACKS FOR BEING POOR

Poverty in the modern United States is a social problem, not an individual failing or a natural disaster. There is no God-given reason why, in a country that has, for so long, been proud to call itself the richest nation on Earth, so many people should be denied the basic necessities of a decent life. When millions are subsisting on or below the poverty line, we are clearly not dealing with a case of the odd individual who wastes the opportunities supposedly provided to all by the free-market economy. Such mass poverty can only be a problem created by the way in which this society produces and distributes its wealth.

Poverty on the scale that exists today is a searing indictment of the American system, a sign of deep-seated inequalities in a democratic society. Deflecting responsibility for this embarrassing state of affairs is a priority for those in power. Their traditional gambit is to try to attach responsibility to the poor themselves and to turn mainstream opinion against those at the bottom of the economic pile. This strategy is far more effective for the authorities if they can attach a distinctive group characteristic to the poor and blame this trait for poor people's problems. Race provides the most potent group characteristic that the elites can exploit for these purposes in our time.

The association of poverty with the alleged characteristics of inner-city Black communities is a classic example of how the race discourse is turning the truth on its head today. The indisputable fact is that as a group, Black Americans make up the poorest of the poor in U.S. society. The question, however, is, how do you explain that fact? In reality, this situation is a result of systematic discrimination against Blacks in America. In the world according to the current wisdom, however, poverty is more the consequence of the failure of Blacks to act like proper Americans. Thus, what ought to be a damning case against a segregated society is twisted into an argument about Blacks' supposed inability to integrate.

As we noted in an earlier chapter, few commentators are as yet prepared to hold Blacks responsible for poverty and inequality on biological grounds. But it is now a commonly accepted notion that certain cultural characteristics of Black communities have held Black people back, and that overcoming these dysfunctional attitudes is crucial to overcoming the problems of the ghetto.

At the heart of the emerging post-liberal consensus is the assumption that the problems of the Black communities of the inner cities are not the responsibility of the American social and economic system. It is not, we are told by academics, pundits, politicians, and experts, a "crude" question of a shortage of government investment or of employers failing to provide job opportunities in the ghetto. Instead, they insist, what is lacking most in the inner city today is "the spirit of enterprise" or "a sense of individual responsibility." Stripped of the jargon, these statements really mean that, one way or another, impoverished Blacks themselves are responsible for combating their dire economic circumstances.

Holding the Black communities of the ghetto responsible for the problems of the inner city serves several overlapping and valuable functions for the business and political elites of the United States. In essence, it relieves the elites of responsibility for tackling poverty and deprivation by turning reality on its head. Instead of admitting that elites have been waging a virtual war on the poor through under-investment and welfare-spending cuts, the post-liberal approach allows the elites to claim that they have spent TOO MUCH on the inner cities, and that over-generous welfare handouts have only encouraged dependency, irresponsibility, and sloth among the poor. This argument paves the way for increasingly severe cuts in welfare payments to the poor. And in the process of criticizing the "dependency culture" among the Black poor, government agencies are able to divert attention from the extent to which they really have subsidized a "dependent" section of society—the parasitically rich elite of corporate America.

Insisting that impoverished Black communities must start taking responsibility for solving their own problems also serves a political function for those who hold the reins of power at the top of American society. It reinforces a political division within the ranks of America's working people, between those deemed "responsible citizens" and those branded as the "irresponsible underclass"—a division that, while discussed in these coded terms, is clearly understood as essentially racial in content. Mobilizing around this divide helps the political elite to break apart any popular opposition among the working classes to welfare and social-service cuts , and to consolidate a "responsible" constituency, that is more receptive to conservative messages on other social issues.

We shall look further at some of the more political aspects of the ideological campaign to blame Blacks, in our examination of the issues of crime and the "underclass." Here the analysis will focus on how, by emphasizing the need for impoverished Blacks to show more responsibility and enterprise, the American business and political elites are better able to explain away

the economic inequalities of race and class, which are an integral part of their system.

THE MEANING OF "PERSONAL RESPONSIBILITY"

"Conservatives have always believed that Blacks and
other minorities would be better served in the long run by
programs that foster independence, rather than those that foster
dependency on government. As so many responsible Black
commentators have noted of late, "We are no longer living in
the sixties. This is the nineties. We need to quit blaming other
people and look to ourselves for self-improvement." That's
right. Though we have not eradicated racism in this country,
conservatives believe that the Blacks' best avenue to success is
through self-reliance."[1]

The words directly above were spoken by populist radio
and TV talk-show host Rush Limbaugh. They represent the
authentic voice of plain-speaking America conservatism. Limbaugh admits that there is still a little racism in the United
States, but only of the red-neck variety. But, he insists, there is
no longer any grounds for sixties-style complaints about institutionalized racism in U.S. society.

"Let's stop exaggerating about the roadblocks to success
in this country," Limbaugh continues. He wants to "remove
artificial barriers to anyone's improvement," but argues that
many of these "reside in the politics of class envy and government dependency." According to Limbaugh, the key to improving the lot of Black people is now known to be, not social change,
but the encouragement of "personal responsibility, self-reliance, and honesty."[2] In other words, if you don't make it, it's
your own fault.

Despite the popularity of his shows, the pugnacious Rush
Limbaugh, with his homespun philosophies, is not usually

considered to be representative of mainstream thought by political commentators. Indeed, he has had more than one skir-
mish with the spokesmen of official America, up to and
including President Bill Clinton himself. Yet the striking thing
is that while Limbaugh's language may be unusually blunt, the
essence of what Limbaugh says about the need for more individual responsibility and self-reliance among impoverished
Blacks, about the need for them to "quit blaming other people,"
is now accepted by most mainstream political thinkers. The
language that the grey men of Washington use to express the
argument may be a bit less colorful than Limbaugh's patois, but
the message is pretty much the same. The cult of individual
responsibility is one of the first principles of political life today.

The bipartisan adherence to that principle was well-illus-
trated in the political response to the Los Angeles riots in the
spring of 1992. There was still riot smoke hanging in the air
when President Bush visited Los Angeles in May. In a speech
delivered at the heart of L.A.'s trouble-spot, he declared his
commitment to put things right in America's cities, to ensure
that things did not return to a situation "where the system
perpetuates failure and hatred and poverty and despair."[3] At
first, it was rather shocking to hear a Republican president
attack "the system" for creating "poverty and despair." As one
account of the speech asks, "Had the devastation Bush witnessed suddenly transformed him into a critic of institutionalized racism and corporate capitalism?" But as the same account
quickly concludes, "Hardly. Bush had something quite different
in mind."[4]

The "system" which Bush blamed for creating poverty and
despair in the inner cities was not corporate capitalism but
liberal welfarism. He argued that the federal government had
spent $3 trillion over 25 years trying to eradicate poverty and
racism but had only succeeded in encouraging dependency and
irresponsible behavior. The solution he proposed was predict-
able and, for those who cared to read between the lines, omi-

nous: "We must start with a set of principles and policies that foster personal responsibility, that refocus entitlement programs to serve those who are most needy." Bush believed that the way in which you "foster personal responsibility" among the "dependent" is clearly by removing the crutch of welfare on which they have been idly and irresponsibly leaning; for "refocus," read "cut."

The Democratic Party's "alternative" to Bush's post-Los Angeles attack upon welfare payments to the inner-city communities demonstrated the consolidation of a post-liberal consensus among the political elite. Democratic presidential contender Bill Clinton did make some liberal-sounding criticisms of the Republicans for cold-shouldering the inner cities and exploiting racial tensions. But when he came to the core argument, it sounded strangely familiar. Many welfare programs of the 1960s had not worked, said Clinton, and future government policies would need to "demand more responsibility" from the urban poor.[5] Other members of the Clinton camp went further, directly echoing Republican demands for an end to "dependency-forming" welfare programs such as Aid for Families with Dependent Children.

For many people, the new emphasis upon "self-reliance" and "individual responsibility" may seem fair enough if accepted at face value. After all, nobody wants to be thought of as irresponsible or as incapable of looking after their own families. Taken out of the context of the current political climate, the notion that people should stand up for themselves and be independent can even sound noble. However, what does it mean when people like Limbaugh or Bush stress the need for inner-city Blacks to be more self-reliant and responsible? It can only mean more cuts in welfare programs for the poor, and even less aid for the inner cities. The fact that candidate Clinton echoed the same sentiments, and has continued to emphasize the message of individual responsibility during his tenure in presidential office, illustrates how far things have gone towards the formation of a post-liberal consensus in American social policy.

A THING OF THE PAST?

It is worth dealing briefly with some of the facts of inequity behind the conservative case, before going on to examine some of the political purposes that the arguments about Black poverty play for the U.S. elites.

There are some important assumptions about contemporary U.S. society underpinning the new emphasis upon the need for Blacks to assume individual responsibility for their welfare. In particular, this emphasis implies that institutionalized discrimination against Black people—in terms of jobs, welfare, education, and so on—is now a problem of the past. Instead, the focus on individual responsibility claims that what undermines Black people today is primarily their own attitudes and outlooks. Telling Black people to be more responsible and self-reliant is another way of saying, "If you are poor or disadvantaged, it must largely be your own fault, because society is not holding you back."

Conservatives will often point to such developments as the abolition of overtly discriminatory laws and the rise of Black politicians and officials as "proof" of the ending of discrimination. Indeed, they now go much further than that. As Rush Limbaugh articulated above, one of the loudest conservative complaints of recent years has been that such measures as affirmative-action programs and quota systems have tipped the balance of regulation far too heavily in favor of Blacks. If there is any racial discrimination in the United States today, they imply, then it is just as likely to operate at the expense of Whites.

The notion that, as Limbaugh puts it, "we are no longer living in the sixties" is central to the current discourse. It points out that the old segregationist system that people fought against back then has gone; and it argues that the welfarism that replaced discrimination in the sixties is now seen as just as problematic for Black people as segregation. In which case, what we need is less carping about social inequality, and more self-reliance.

Everybody can agree with this argument up to a point. It is undoubtedly profoundly true that we are not living in the sixties, as a glance at any calendar will readily confirm. But so what? Exactly what is it that has changed so fundamentally for Black people in the United States over the past three decades as to make inequality and discrimination things of the past?

It is undeniable that formal slavery has been abolished, that the Constitution of the United States of America no longer says that a Black man is worth two-thirds of a White man, and that racial segregation in many areas of life has been outlawed. However, there often seems to be little relationship between what the law formally declares and the way in which the authorities actually operate. Tell Black youths who have suffered at the hands of the police and courts about the benefits of the Bill of Rights. Ask the Black sharecroppers of the South how far their dignity is protected by civil rights bills and the Supreme Court.

The fact that rights are written into law does not necessarily mean that they are exercised in practice. All manner of social and economic mechanisms and pressures can combine to make sure that they are not. Similarly, the fact that there is no current law that states that Blacks are second class citizens does not mean that discrimination is a thing of the past.

The merest glance at the reality confronting the majority of Blacks daily suggests that, in every corner of life and every sphere of political and economic activity, modern American society continues to operate a systematic (though unwritten) code of racial discrimination. Indeed, far from racial discrimination being a relic of history, some of the latest trends would suggest that racial discrimination is, if anything, a growing threat to the rights and living standards of Black (and increasingly Latino) Americans.

There is no shortage of hard evidence with which to demonstrate the prevalence and disproportionate concentration of deprivation within the Black communities of the inner cities. For instance, an astounding 43 percent of all Black children in America today live in poverty—and at around 18 deaths per thousand births, the Black infant mortality rate in the United States is more than double the average for Whites. It is also higher than the rate for some third world countries.[6] In 1990, the median income for a Black family had been estimated at $21,423. For a White family in the same year, the figure works out at $36,915—more than 70 percent higher.[7]

Hacker has marshalled various statistics from the official U.S. census to show that the majority of American Blacks continue to get the worst of life in every area, from employment and income to health and education. His table on family-income distribution demonstrates most forcefully the economic disparity between the races.

The figures on annual income for Black and White families are like mirror images of one another. Whereas the largest group of Whites (32.5 percent) is in the $50,000-plus bracket, and the smallest section of the White population (16.5 percent) has an income under $15,000, for Blacks it is almost the exact opposite. Just 14.5 percent of Black families have an income of more than $50,000, compared with 37 percent who get under $15,000 a year. What these figures indicate is that while talk of the creation of a new Black middle class may be somewhat justified, that small section of the Black population is massively outnumbered by those with low and very low incomes. At 37 percent, the proportion of families with an annual income of less than $15,000 is easily the largest group of Blacks (and it is proportionately far larger than any section of the White population).[8]

Even these figures tend to underestimate the differentials in income between the White and Black middle classes. Not only are there far more White families earning more than $50,000 a year, but they are also far more likely to be made up of a husband earning $75,000 and a wife who stays at home. By contrast, in those relatively few Black families that manage an income of $50,000-plus, as Hacker argues elsewhere, "the husband is likely to be a bus driver earning $32,000, while his wife brings home $28,000 as a teacher or a nurse."[9]

Of course, the nineties really are not the sixties. There have been some significant changes in the patterns of Black employment. There is no longer any occupation, for example, where an absolute color bar operates. Some Black faces can be found in every area of the economy. But "some" can mean very few. The forms of inequality have merely been modified and modernized—not abolished.

Despite all the publicity given to the rise of the professional Black middle classes, for example, Blacks are still badly underrepresented in professions such as engineering, law, medicine, architecture, and journalism. And they are considerably overrepresented in many of the more low-paid, menial, and mindnumbing occupations—not only traditional ones, like nursing orderlies or janitors or postal clerks, but also the nineties-style drudgery of working as data-entry keyers or telephone operators.

The continued influence of discriminatory attitudes in shaping employment patterns is also demonstrated in less obvious ways than the shortage of Blacks in top professions. For example, Black workers are still scarce in some fairly menial jobs where employees have to make contact with customers. Black people make up less than 5 percent of waiters and waitresses, and only around 3.5 percent of bartenders. What is the explanation for such under-representation? Not lack of qualifications on the part of Black applicants, that's for sure. It can only be that employers do not want their restaurants or bars "tarnished" by being seen as Black or "colored." Little things like this powerfully demonstrate that Black people continue to be viewed and treated as second-class citizens in the United States and its labor markets.[10]

REALITIES AND PERCEPTIONS

It may seem unnecessary to spell out the basic facts about institutionalized discrimination in an analysis such as ours. After all, many of these statistics are readily available elsewhere. Yet it is important to begin by outlining the real pattern of discrimination in the U.S. economy and labor markets, in order to throw into sharp relief the distorted view of reality that is given by the current debate about race and equality.

In a different time and context, the systematic character of the problems of inequality facing Black people might be taken as irrefutable evidence of a fundamental flaw in the structures of American society. But not today. The way in which the elites of the political and media worlds have manipulated the race issue has ensured that American public opinion is left with a very different impression—one entirely at variance with the facts.

In the first place, many Americans no longer believe that there is a genuine economic inequality between races in the United States. The conservative elite has bombarded society with the argument that segregation has been abolished and that positive discrimination has actually bestowed economic privileges on Black people. As a consequence, many people now dismiss allegations of discrimination against Blacks as a thing of the past. In a 1989 survey, conducted by Louis Harris and Associates, for example, nearly half of the White Americans polled believed that Blacks were as well off as Whites; in the same survey, fewer than 20 percent of Black respondents believed that the races were economically equal. The subsequent development of the debate about race and poverty suggests that the disparity in responses is likely to be even wider today.

In the second place, insofar as economic inequality *is* still recognized, it is no longer seen in the way that it was widely interpreted thirty years ago, i.e., as a consequence of a segregated system. Instead, there is an increasingly hostile tendency to ascribe the problems of inequality to a fundamental flaw in the cultural and psychological makeup of Black people themselves.

This, then, is what has really changed most dramatically from the sixties to the nineties: not the facts of discrimination and inequality but the way in which Black problems are perceived and discussed under the influence of more elitist ideologies.

By setting out the facts about the contemporary patterns of racial discrimination, we can demonstrate that the new consensus around issues of race and poverty is an ideological construction of the elites. It becomes clear that these views reflect, not the *social reality* of continuing poverty and discrimination, but the dominant *political perceptions* that have been instilled from the top down by powerful elites capable of constructing an interpretative consensus that flies in the face of the facts.

But statistics alone are not a sufficient response to the case against the Black poor. It is now necessary to look at the role that these arguments play for the political and business elites in U.S. society. Demonstrating the manipulative and self-serving character of the race discourse is an important first step towards cracking open the post-liberal consensus.

WHOSE DEPENDENCY CULTURE?

The powerful act of truth-reversal that has been achieved in relation to perceptions of the Black poor serves several interlocking functions for the American elites. All of these distorted arguments about race and poverty have in common that they serve to mystify the true extent and causes of all the class and racial inequalities in American society, and so they lend legitimacy to the existing economic order on which the elites depend for their privileges.

Take, for example, the modern conservative case against welfare payments. The basic argument is that poor Blacks have been reduced to their current state by a combination of their own "ghetto culture" and the misguided interventions of White liberal do-gooders with government welfare programs.

Indeed, there is a growing tendency to identify the inner-city problems of the 1990s as a partial consequence of the attempted inner-city solutions of the 1960s. According to this aspect of the conservative world view, sixties aid programs—such as the Great Society and the War on Poverty—only helped to sow the seeds of the current crisis in the ghettos. These liberal programs allegedly laid the foundation for the "welfare dependency" which now afflicts the inner cities and which conservatives claim has brought with it all the problems of single-parent families, immorality, sloth, crime, and drugs. Thus the liberal-sponsored response to the riots and unrest of the sixties is held at least partly responsible for bringing about the Los Angeles riots of 1992.

All of these arguments from White and Black conservatives meet in their insistence that market forces and more free enterprise hold the economic key to improving the lot of the Blacks at the bottom of the American ladder. The flipside of this argument is that welfare programs should be cut back to "free" the poor from the so-called culture of poverty and the scourge of dependency.

However, the entire case against welfare put forward by the conservative elites is based upon a cynically twisted misrepresentation of the real relationship between poverty, business enterprise, and government intervention in the cities of the

United States. The effect of this misrepresentation is, on one hand, to disguise and excuse the government's war against the poor and, on the other, to divert attention from the massive hand-outs with which government agencies have propped up the business elites.

This misrepresentation is reinforced with vicious stereotypes. For example, many Republican politicians (and a growing number of Democrats) can be heard expounding upon the problem posed by "welfare queens" in the ghettos. The language some of them use conjures up images of indulgence and pampering, of Black "queens" living off welfare checks (and probably off crack cocaine too), surrounded by illegitimate offspring who will grow up to take their place in the ghetto cycle of dependency and criminality—or perhaps to take the job of a better-qualified White by exploiting the affirmative-action and quota programs sponsored by the interfering liberals. Conservatives like to contrast all of this rottenness and decay of the dependency culture to the supposed vibrancy and dynamism of the free-market economy, where they claim people can get ahead regardless of color by making the most of their talents and opportunities. The obvious solution to Black poverty thus becomes more free markets, enterprise, and competition and less easy welfare and fewer subsidies.

These arguments can sound particularly moral and persuasive when put forward by the spokesmen of Black conservatism. In the eighties, for example, the thoughts of Black economist Thomas Sowell, a disciple of Milton Freidman's free-market school at the University of Chicago, came very much into fashion. Sowell's argument is that Black people and the members of other minority communities in America do better in laissez-faire economic systems than in systems where the government intervenes extensively in the economy.[11]

It all sounds straightforward enough, until you look a little more closely at the reality of both life in the inner cities and the way in which the American economy operates. It then becomes clear that the ghettos and the people who live there get far too little, not too much, in the way of public support and access to the resources of society. It should also become clear that one reason for this shortfall is the way in which the authorities prioritize public spending on projects that will subsidize the wealthy corporations of the "free" market business sector. Indeed, if there is a pervasive "dependency culture" in the United States today, it is centered upon massive government support for the elite directors and shareholders of ailing industries, banks, and businesses. By focusing public debate on "welfare dependency" in the ghetto, the spokesmen for elite interests ensure that the issue of corporate subsidies, which exposes many of the myths of free-market economics, is kept out of the political spotlight.

The image of the Black and Latino communities of the inner cities somehow having been "spoiled" by welfare and public-spending programs since the sixties would be laughable if it were not so dangerous. At every turn, the inner cities have been denied the resources they need. And the situation is not getting any better; the majority of Blacks are having to cope with fewer jobs, lower real welfare payments, worse housing, schools, and hospitals, and a dirtier living environment.

The inner-city areas of a major city like Los Angeles (primarily South Central and Koreatown) provide graphic examples of the reality behind all of the rhetoric about "dependency." One local study backed by the Los Angeles Labor/Community Strategy Center has spelled out the true state of affairs:

"More needful of social services than other communities because of the lack of jobs, South Central in fact gets less, and many are from agencies outside the traditional government apparatus. Basic needs are not being met by state, county, or city agencies. Some sections of the 9th District have never been visited by the Bureau of Sanitation's regular weekly trash trucks and street sweepers. This is a neighborhood where individuals and families try desperately to solve their problems alone because there is little or no help."[12]

Conservative commentators regularly imply (and others often accept) that the inner cities have been a bottomless pit swallowing up a greater and greater share of public money since the sixties. The irony is that the reverse is closer to the truth. In fact, the War on Poverty and other federal spending initiatives were very short-lived and pretty superficial. For example, even at their height, the youth job-creation programs launched in the sixties often looked more like public-relations exercises than genuine social initiatives. But even those small employment initiatives which existed have been progressively cut back or done away with altogether. In more recent times, the Los Angeles city authorities begrudgingly agreed to one $0.5 million pilot program to create 100 jobs for "high-risk" youth in 1988. At that time, the Los Angeles Police Department was receiving more than $400 million a year to control and contain those same youths with paramilitary tactics and technology. Housing programs have gone the same way as the employment schemes. Only two days before the 1992 Los Angeles riots broke out, a city council committee voted to take away almost $50 million earmarked for its Community Redevelopment Agency's low-income housing program and use it instead to pay for extra police and fire services!

There is a similar story of under-investment to be told in every branch of public services. The Black ghettos have higher infant mortality rates, higher death rates from cancer, heart and liver diseases, and higher rates of influenza and pneumonia than other population centers. Yet health care budgets have been slashed and trauma centers closed across the inner cities. And education facilities have fallen apart as cash-conscious authorities create "children's ghettos" of crowded, disadvantaged schools in the poorest, predominantly Black and Latino districts.

The deteorioration of social services has become part of a generalized and all-party assault on welfare spending for the poor in America's cities. Indeed, federal government support for major cities has been savaged. Between 1980 and 1992, federal aid was cut by almost two-thirds, costing cities an estimated $26 billion a year (in constant 1990 dollars)[13] Cities like New York, Los Angeles, and Philadelphia have been left to lurch from one financial crisis to another, their administrations trying to make ends meet through regressive sales taxes that hit the poor hardest and huge budget cuts that cost the inner-city communities dearly in jobs and services. There has been more bad news at the state levels, where Democrat-run legislatures have slashed health and welfare spending and made it harder to claim benefits. The Republicans, elected to run many states in 1994, promised even deeper cuts in social spending.

The notion that impoverished Black communities are being indulged in modern America is thus a gross distortion of the truth. Far from being "spoiled" by welfare profligacy, the lives of poor Black people are being ruined by what amounts to an economic war on the poor, a war waged by those in power at every level of the American system.

The shift of resources away from Black and Latino inner-city communities in recent years partly reflects the rise of the political influence of the largely White residential suburbs, where more public spending has been directed. However, there is also another reason why not just Reagan and Bush but the Los Angeles administration of Black reforming mayor Tom Bradley saw fit to deprive areas like South Central of desperately needed resources. They have funnelled financial support into propping up the corporate elite of U.S. business. At the federal level, billions of dollars of public money have gone directly or indirectly into corporate coffers, particularly in the defense and, more recently, the banking sectors. At the local level, public investment in the cities has been concentrated in hand-outs to urban developers of one kind or another.

Public money *has* been spent in the cities. But instead of making social investments, the authorities at federal, state, and city levels have prioritized the use of resources to subsidize wealthy business interests—in effect, to prop up the "free" market, which seems to have become increasingly "dependent" upon such government support.

For example, urban development in Los Angeles has always been effectively controlled by high-powered business interests—bankers, real estate owners, corporate executives—organized in groups like the Committee of Twenty-Five or the LA 2000 Committee. They have used their considerable influence over local government to shape the city in their own image, often with the sizeable support of public money. So while low-cost-housing construction programs were being cancelled in the seventies, government aid to commercial development was being increased.

This bias towards business interests in the distribution of public funds has reached almost obscene proportions in recent years. While spending on the Black and Latino areas of the inner city has been squeezed tighter and tighter, and requests for more resources have been rejected out of hand, the Bradley administration adopted the big-business development agenda for the Central City Association. More than $2 billion of city money went to subsidizing the financial and commercial sector redevelopments in downtown Los Angeles as part of this project. This new fortress-style city-within-a-city, all shining office towers and high-security shopping malls, has been built by developers, speculators, and corporate chiefs, with the massive assistance of a hand-out from the public purse—at the same time that those business interests and the politicians whom they sponsor have been railing against the evils of welfare for the Black and Latino poor.

In other words, more than $2 billion has been handed out to a relative handful of some of the richest and most powerful people in Los Angeles. Meanwhile, those countless thousands at the other end of the social scale, in the Black ghettos of South Central, have become yet more disadvantaged, even falling behind some other, better-off areas of the city when it comes to receiving anti-poverty assistance. If that is not a clear-cut example of officially endorsed economic discrimination, what is?

For all this evidence, this pattern of blatant discrimination against the urban poor in favor of the corporate elite has not become a real issue of public debate. A large part of the explanation for this oversight lies in the manipulation of the race issue and the politicization of the racial divide to serve the self-indulgent elite. The mouthpieces of the American elites have successfully connected White concerns about where the government spends their tax dollars to the question of the racial divide, and thus have turned public hostility against the ghetto. The political and business elites, who are involved in multi-billion dollar hand-outs and in creating a culture of dependency, are not only let off the hook; they are also left free to lecture the Black poor about their alleged parasitism towards the public purse.

The Black ghetto pays a heavy price for the elites' manipulation of the arguments around "dependency." The urban Black communities are not only the poorest of America's poor. They are also the section of the poor that is increasingly blamed for creating their own problems and for swallowing billions of dollars in government hand-outs. Institutionalized racial discrimination does not only deny impoverished Blacks the resources they desperately need; it also seeks to justify that denial to the rest of America as a consequence of the "culture of poverty" in the Black ghetto. As a result, it sets the scene for further, deeper cuts in spending on welfare and social services in the urban wasteland.

WHITES PAY A PRICE

The carefully cultivated myth that impoverished Blacks have had it easy since the 1960s also plays an additional and very useful role for the U.S. elites. It has helped them to consolidate a powerful conservative bloc among working White Americans. Conservative spokesmen in the political and press worlds have put a lot of effort into popularizing the idea that affirmative-action programs and quota systems rooted in the sixties reforms have reversed racial discrimination, by boosting the job and income prospects of unqualified Blacks at the expense of Whites. The issue of affirmative action and quotas has become a political weapon, preying on the real economic insecurities among Whites that have been created, not by Black privilege, but by the market economy managed by the truly privileged elite. After the November 1994 Congressional elections, Gingrich's Republican crusaders put affirmative action programs at the top of their hit list.

Once again, it is useful to set out the disparity between the image of positive discrimination and the reality, in order to demonstrate the manipulative character of the conservative case against such policies. The fact is that, in practice, these measures have made little or no difference to the relative positions of the vast majority of Black employees. For example, it has been estimated that, at the start of the 1980s, the average Black male was paid $715 for every $1,000 earned by his average White counterpart. By the end of that decade—a decade where affirmative action programs are said to have priveleged Black workers over White workers—that figure has risen by one dollar, to $716 per $1,000.[14]

Thus, the conservative arguments about positive discrimination and quotas being the scourge of the White working man bear little or no relation to reality. Yet that has not prevented those arguments from becoming a potent political tool in the service of the social elites, a tool that they have used to divide the workforce along racial lines, thus hindering any potential popular opposition. This success reflects the extent to which the conservatives have managed both to connect with many Whites' own concerns about their deteriorating job prospects and falling real wages and to use the prism of race to focus that anger and bitterness against Blacks alleged to be profiting at their expense.

The cruel irony is that the issue of falling pay levels brings out a definite common interest among Black and White sections of the American workforce. To one degree or another, each has been a victim of the determination of the corporate elite to boost its profit levels—if necessary, at the expense of employees' jobs, pay, and working conditions. For example, from 1979 to 1989, the real annual earnings of low-skilled White men in their twenties fell by 14 percent. But far from profiting from this process, their Black counterparts saw their income cut by 24 percent. White male high school drop-outs in their twenties are estimated to have lost up to HALF of their real incomes over the same period.[15] And whatever claims may be made on behalf of the new Black middle classes, the unimpressive impact of affirmative action on the overall picture can surely best be illustrated by the fact that, even in a time of recession, when White employees incomes were decreasing, Black workers' earnings were continuing to fall faster and farther.

Yet the prospect of a unified resistance to wage cuts never really existed. The top-down politicization of the racial divide through the campaign against affirmative action saw to that. The manipulation of racially charged issues has thus served to insulate the business elites from popular pressure, and to help the conservative political elite consolidate a base of support among White working Americans.

So far we have tried to establish how the problems caused by systematic discrimination and by the operation of an economic framework that consistently puts corporate profit before the needs of an impoverished community have been disguised and legitimized through the discourse on race and poverty. Let us now turn briefly to examine how this relates to two of the more fashionable "solutions" for the inner cities, that have been suggested by various Black and White conservatives since the 1992 Los Angeles riots.

THE ENTERPRIZE ZONE ILLUSION

Over the past few years, a fashionable solution for the inner cities put forward by businesss and political commentators has been to argue that the ghettos can be revitalized by creating more of a business culture there (preferably built around Black business, something we will examine in a later chapter). One proposal that has come to the fore since the 1992 Los Angeles riots is for the extension of enterprize zones in the inner city.

The idea of encouraging business in the inner cities by creating new enterprise zones has been put forward by conservatives for a decade. It has been taken up more seriously in Washington since the Los Angeles riots, and now figures prominently in the Democrats' agenda too. The theory is that by offering tax-breaks to companies that start up in desolate areas, enterprize zones can help to kick-start the inner-city economies back to life.

In fact, there is no reason to suppose that enterprize zones can do anything practical to alleviate the problems of the Black ghetto. But that is not the primary function of the campaign anyway. By emphasizing the need for a little more free-market acumen (and a little lower pay) in the inner cities, the authorities and economists pushing for more enterprize zones are broadcasting an important ideological message on behalf of the powers that be. The message is that the problems of the ghetto are internal ones, which could be solved if only the people there would shrug off their slothful ways and show more enterprise.

Over the past decade or so, 38 states have created more than 600 enterprise zones in their inner cities. Yet the zones have made little discernible difference to the people of the blighted areas they encompass. Companies will only move to an inner-city area if it makes sense according to the same criterion by which they judge everything—the drive to maximize profits. And that criterion is not necessarily compatible with the primary needs of the area's impoverished and predominantly Black and Latino populations. As one local study notes of South Central LA's previous experience of publicly subsidized business development:

"Financiers, real estate interests and politicians have been supporting investment that increases the value of land and from which a profit can be made. Using these criteria, a strategically-placed parking lot can be considered a better investment than low-income housing. It is no accident, therefore, that the limited development South Central has experienced has been commercial. These become 'low-risk' investments for outsiders because of the assistance offered by CRA and the city, which includes assembling land to create larger parcels (using the power of condemnation)."[16]

Any development based upon the creation of new enterprise zones would be likely to follow a similarly unproductive pattern for local people. Most high-tech manufacturers, for example, are unwilling to open new plants in inner-city areas. Those firms which do move into enterprize zones to take advantage of the tax breaks often hire skilled workers from outside the communities. For instance, one custom-metal fabricator in the Benton Harbor (Michigan) enterprize zone, where local unemployment runs at 28 percent, has conceded that 60 percent of its workforce came from outside the city.[17]

Encouraged by federal policy, factory owners seeking cheap sites and labor are most likely to utilize the labor of *maquiladoras,* factories in the Mexican border manufacturing region where wages average 50 CENTS AN HOUR. Against that background, the sort of rock-bottom wages that an enterprise-zone sweatshop boss would need to pay to compete are hardly likely to relieve the ghetto's dire poverty. For instance, in the aftermath of the 1992 riots, Disney said that it might build a factory in South Central LA—and might pay the California minimum wage of $4.25 an hour. That generous offer would instantly place a full-time worker at a level 25 percent below the official poverty line.

So what exactly would the Black and Latino communities gain from the kind of subsidized business development that they have been promised through the prospect of enterprise zones? The most obvious thing they get is big new shopping malls, built and owned by corporate syndicates (with city support). If they are "lucky," local Black and Latino people might get a job serving in one of the new stores. Which is why in South Los Angeles, as veteran trade unionist and writer Richard Rothstein has pointed out, the "fastest growing occupation is now 'salesperson,' with an average entry wage of $4.75 an hour."[18] Young Blacks might just get such a poverty-waged job; but if they are among the many who do not, they will find it hard even to walk through "their" new shopping centers without attracting the intrusive attentions of security guards and video surveillance cameras.

The proposal for more enterprise zones typifies the official response to the latest crisis in the American inner city. It involves no practical government action or investment, other than the offer of some tax breaks to businesses on the lookout for cheap labor. It leaves the prospects of the inner-city communities in the hands of a market economy that offers them poverty-level wages as something to which they should aspire. And above all, it tells the impoverished people of the ghettos to stop moaning about welfare cuts and unemployment and sort out their own problems by showing a bit more "enterprise."

As a practical solution to the economic plight of the inner cites, enterprise zones are thus a non-starter. But as a political device to strengthen the post-liberal consensus about the causes of Black poverty and reinforce the trend to scapegoat the ghetto, the calls for more enterprise zones can be seen as another useful message on behalf of the powerful and propertied elites.

"MOVE WHERE THE JOBS ARE"

It is much the same story with another market-oriented "solution" that has been proposed by supporters of the post-liberal consensus—the notion that welfare should be cut so as to force the urban poor to get off their butts and leave the ghetto for good in search of work. This solution would apparently leave the inner cities free for the public-spirited developers and construction corporations who can make them great again.

This is a proposal that encapsulates the elitist character of the core economic arguments now being discussed in relation to ghetto communities. It suggests that the problems of poverty, bad housing, and unemployment are essentially caused by the sloth of the Black communities themselves, and that the best thing the authorities can do for these people is to relieve them of the burden of receiving welfare so that they can be free to make something of their lives. An old-fashioned proposal for hammering the poor, in order to save the wealthy and the government money, is here transformed into a benevolent act to save poor Black people from themselves. That is the beauty of the post-liberal consensus on the relationship between race and poverty from the perspective of the economic and political elites of contemporary America.

The proposal that Blacks should leave the inner city and go forth to make their fortunes in America might sound like the sort of conservative fantasy scenario associated with the likes of Rush Limbaugh. But some of the most forceful advocates of this plan like Clinton aide Mickey Kaus, author of *The End of Equality*, have actually come from among the New Democrats. Kaus has used these arguments to support the case against welfare payments: "Welfare may not have been the main cause of the underclass, but it enabled the underclass to form. Without welfare, those left behind in the ghetto would have to move where the jobs were."[19]

The argument is that instead of lazing around in the ghettos on welfare, Blacks should simply pull up stakes and move to where the jobs are. This might sound like a straightforward enough idea. But there is one small detail that Kaus and his co-thinkers ignore. The jobs have often quite deliberately been moved to where the Blacks are NOT.

The attempt to "move to where the jobs [were]" was, of course, what prompted many thousands of Black people to relocate from the South to Los Angeles and other cities in the first place. After the Second World War, inner-city Los Angeles was an industrial hub, its factories producing airplane parts and Buick cars and creating jobs for incoming Black workers. Even in LA's industrial heyday, Blacks suffered badly from discrimination; those who managed to get jobs in the steelworks outside of town, for example, invariably found themselves working in the inferno of the cooking ovens. It is a mark of how far things have deteriorated in recent years that such times can now be looked back upon as "good old days."

From the mid-1970s onwards, the traditional industries that had employed Blacks in Los Angeles and elsewhere in California collapsed. Close to 75,000 blue-collar jobs disappeared between 1978 and 1982 alone, as ten of the dozen biggest non-aerospace plants in California closed. Any small advances that Black workers might have made in the previous decade were wiped out, as unemployment in South Central Los Angeles rose to almost 50 percent. As the new, often defense-related industries grew up in California, they avoided the old inner-city areas of Los Angeles and relocated out in the suburbs. And "suburban" meant largely White.

To listen to some conservatives talk, you would think that Blacks had remained in the inner-city ghettos on welfare out of choice, that they had turned down the opportunity to move to the leafy suburbs and get good jobs. The truth is that from the time large-scale suburbanization began in the 1920s, it was organized along racially exclusive lines to deliberately create all-White residential strongholds—with the full support of U.S. government agencies. As we have argued in Chapter Two, this segregationist strategy has been further developed and made more sophisticated in recent years.

Seen from this perspective, the character of government-sponsored suburbanization—the "White flight"— along with public housing policies, has clearly trapped many Blacks and Latinos in the inner-city ghettos of cities such as Los Angeles, whether they like it or not. Even those relatively few middle-class Black families who can afford to move out have often had to create all-Black suburbs of their own. Several studies suggest that the process of suburbanization can tend to break down the traditional ethnic divisions among White communities; but it seems only to harden the racial segregation between Black and White.

With much of the Black population stuck in the inner cities, many of those who make decisions about employment and economic development appear to have pursued a deliberate policy of moving to where the Blacks are not. While the suburbs enjoyed an extended service-sector boom in the Reagan eighties, areas like South Central just keep on getting poorer.

The scale of the economic discrimination facing Blacks in America's cities today suggests that their problems are unlikely to be solved simply by getting on a subsidized bus to go and look for a job. The only practical consequence of the arguments put forward by people like Mickey Kaus is to justify further cuts in sorely needed welfare payments. The political consequence of this New Democrats' crusade is to add a new legitimacy to the system of institutionalized discrimination that has built and maintained the ghettos.

If the "solutions" offered by business interests and their political supporters could not emancipate Black Americans at the height of the postwar economic boom, then what do they really expect these notions to achieve today, when corporate capitalism has hit such hard times in the United Sates and around the world? Telling Black people to "move where the jobs are" is a particularly sick joke when it should be obvious that the decent, full-time jobs are not really anywhere in 1990s America, and that many of those jobs which are there will be closed to Blacks from the ghetto. Moving out of the cities can do little or nothing to free Black people from the problem of inequality; that is a political problem, not a geographic one. As one character in a recent film about ghetto life says when turning down the chance to move from Watts in LA to the supposed safety of Atlanta, "I'd still be Black."[20]

4. CRIME: "IT'S ALWAYS THE BLACK MAN"

Crime panics are at the heart of the politicization of the racial divide in modern America. We have already established in an earlier discussion the manner in which the manipulation of race by the authorities connects with the aspirations and insecurities of White Americans to give racial hostility far more force and importance than simple prejudice could ever achieve. Nowhere is this trend for elites to distort and exploit genuine popular fears clearer than in relation to crime issues.

Crime, of course, is not some kind of fiction, dreamt up by highly placed conspirators to dupe the public. It is a grim reality of life in the American city that some people do get robbed, beaten, and shot. However, the notion that there is a relentlessly rising tide of violent crime in the United States is a myth. What has been rising rapidly in recent years is not so much the incidence of violent crime itself but the public consciousness of crime as a problem and a political issue. The fear of crime is often wildly disproportionate to the real threat posed. And that consciousness and fear of crime has not only become exaggerated; it has also been distorted into a racial issue.

In a special report entitled "Crime: a conspiracy of silence," *Newsweek* noted how "for many Americans, the law-and-order issue is intertwined with unspoken fears about young Black men."[1] The key word here is "unspoken." On the surface of public life, the raging debate is all about how to deal with criminals, not Black people; but all sides understand that the silent subtext of the law-and-order issue is about race.

This powerful association between Black people and crime in the public mind has not developed spontaneously. The political, media, and intellectual elites have played a key role in turning Black crime into the focus for public fears. Through promoting everything from sensationalized crime stories on the television news to high-profile law-and-order policies on Capitol Hill, these forces have established the image of a criminal Black urban "underclass" threatening civilization and the American way of life.

What the U.S. elites have achieved in the crime debate is to distort the relationship between Black communities and the forces of law and order. In the worldview that these elites have popularized, the problem is violent Black criminals and their gun-and-drug culture. It is Black males, rather than the powerful agents of the American state, who are branded as the aggressors against society, the threat to decent citizens, "the barbarians" at the gate. It follows from this attitude of identifying Black criminals as the cause of society's problems that the strongarm policing methods and sentencing policies adopted in U.S. inner cities over recent years can be presented as a necessary response to that threat, an attempt to constrain the problem on society's behalf. The argument goes like this: if it was not for the criminal tendencies of Black males in the ghetto, there would be no need for the raids, the roadblocks, and the general atmosphere of living under a police army of occupation in America's inner cities today.

These arguments put matters back to front. The real problem begins, not with the so-called criminal pathology of Black ghetto males, but with the structures of U.S. society and the state power that presides over them on behalf of the dominant elites. The preoccupation with crime, I will argue here, is an ideological construction that serves the interests of the elites in a double sense: it disguises the real reasons for the conditions of brutality and repression in the inner cities, thus shifting responsibility away from those in power; and it helps to consolidate a base of support for the law-and-order authorities among White Americans. In this way the government preys on White insecurities and twists them into a racially charged fear of violent Black people.

BLACK AND BLUE

The mainstream contemporary view is that many Black males in urban areas are potentially violent criminals. As a consequence, the police forces of the United States are still widely perceived as a "thin blue line" which, whatever its imperfections, is holding back the tide of barbarism that threatens to swamp "decent" American society. When social unrest among the Black or Latino poor periodically breaks out in the ghetto, it is generally interpreted as proof of the correctness of this view of the relationship between the ghetto communities and the forces of law and order.

The 1992 riots in Los Angeles were a case in point. The fact that these disturbances were caused by the acquittal of police officers filmed brutally beating an unarmed Black civilian was soon forgotten in the rush to condemn the violent criminality of the ghetto. Jim Sleeper, author of *The Closest of Strangers: Liberalism and the Politics of Race in New York*, noted the "self-fulfilling" character of the established belief in Black criminality in these circumstances, and pointed out the divisive conclusions that would be drawn from seeing that view of the problem confirmed:

"We're at the dividing line now, where perception becomes reality, where the prophecy becomes self-fulfilling. The fact that the looters are out there doing the rioting only confirms what people have decided: that this is what the cops are here to protect us from."[2]

However, the problem begins not with Black males but with institutionalized segregation in U.S. society. It is this system of segregation and racial discrimination that both perpetuates the brutality of the ghetto, and gives rise to the repressive policing methods necessary to cope with the consequences of a divided society. The preoccupation with crime is a device that serves to disguise the real roots of the U.S. economic crisis, and to legitimize the process of policing the racial divide.

The largely informal but powerful system of top-down segregation in contemporary America sentences the vast majority of Blacks to live on the margins of society. The evidence of this marginalization can be seen in almost every walk of life: in the ghetto's lack of a political voice, its economic destitution, its social ostracization. Analyzing the extent of residential segregation in American urban areas today, Massey and Denton have gone so far as to suggest that "within a large, diverse, and highly mobile post-industrial society such as the United States, Blacks living in the ghetto are among the most isolated people on Earth."[3]

The degree of isolation and marginalization endured by the impoverished Black communities of the inner cities has far-reaching consequences. On the one hand, it is instrumental in perpetuating the brutalizing conditions of life in the ghetto, which lead to a constant struggle for survival and make violence as inevitable as hunger. On the other hand, the marginalization of the inner city communities by the American social system turns these people into a policing problem from the elitist perspective of the authorities.

The inability of the American economic system to integrate the majority of Blacks leaves them as outsiders, as the "other" in American life. Unable or unwilling to break the cycle of segregation, the U.S. authorities are faced with the need to control the Black communities of the ghetto, to contain them at the margins of society within the barren space left for them by institutionalized discrimination. The hardline, repressive policing methods developed in the inner cities are the result of this elitist strategy of containment and control.

The policing of the ghetto is thus not a response to a rising tide of violent Black crime. It is a proactive attempt to keep these communities in line, to ensure that the Black poor know their place at the bottom and on the borders of U.S. society. The official police forces and the armies of private security officers that occupy the urban battleground operate on the assumption that Blacks, and particularly young Black males, are a public order problem, to be kept down and out—down in the ghetto and out of the shopping malls and space-age city business centers. That attitude has been popularized at every level of American society from the top down, through a concerted campaign by the political and legal authorities, backed up by powerful media voices, which have turned inner-city crime into the constantly running top story of our times.

The crime panic provides the ruling elites with a coded justification for the ruthless policing of Black lives in the inner city. By giving the crime issue an unspoken but pervasive racial element, the authorities have made acceptable the kind of law-and-order war against a section of the population that could otherwise be widely considered unacceptable in a democratic nation. It is the racially charged character of the issue that has allowed the authorities to turn things on their head so successfully and present the Black poor as an aggressive threat to society.

But the crime panic does more for the ruling elites than to simply offer them an excuse for using repressive policing methods to contain and control the marginalized urban ghettos. It also acts as a device that they can use to consolidate support for the forces of state power within the ranks of ordinary White Americans. The message from the political, legal, and media elites today is that crime—and, by implication, Black criminals—represents the major threat to decent Americans. That is a powerful message with which the elites can seek to divert attention away from the crisis of the social and economic system, and to galvanize support and acceptance for the police, the courts, and other key power structures in the United States.

"THEY WANT WHAT YOU'VE GOT"

How do the elites achieve this trick? It is important to stress again that this feat is not a crude question of highly placed conspirators whipping up hysteria about crime out of thin air. The basis for the success of the crime panic, as a political tool of the elites, is rooted in the real social and economic insecurities experienced by so many White Americans in recent years. Sections of the American population, which thought that they had seen the last of the bad old days of depression and fear, have felt themselves being dragged back towards the precipice by the shocking experience of recession, coupled with the removal of many of the old political certainties of the Cold War era. Jobs that were supposed to be "for life" have disappeared overnight. Paychecks that were supposed to provide a consistently rising standard of living have been cut back, and sometimes slashed in half. Most potently of all, the future of White America's children has become increasingly uncertain.

The conviction that your children will be better off than you, just as you are better off than your parents, has in many ways provided the motor force behind the American dream during the past half-century or more. Now, however, there are generations of Americans facing up to the cold fact that this accepted truth no longer holds good. Many parents now recognize that the only way their children will own the kind of family home that every White American once expected as his or her right will be to inherit it upon their death.

These developments have bred deep fears about what is to become of individuals and their families. Many White suburbanites now feel themselves under siege from forces that they can neither understand nor repel. The resulting insecurities have proved fertile ground for the development of the panic about Black crime, under the manipulation of those with authority and influence.

In the racially charged climate of contemporary America, it is not too difficult for the elites to turn White suburban insecurities into fear of crime and hostility towards the Black ghetto. It is easy to get people to identify their problems with what appears to be an immediate and physical threat at hand, rather than to search for less obvious social forces at work. The marginalized, impoverished Black males of the inner cities are clearly outsiders at the gates of the besieged communities of suburban America. It is therefore straightforward enough for those with the power to shape public opinion to point to the "underclass" as a threat, to set up urban Blacks as an outlaw group *that wants to take what White America has got*—to take it either indirectly, through welfare demands on tax dollars, or directly, through violent crime. In this way the anger of insecure White suburbanites can be directed at least partly against the Black ghetto, and away from the market economy, which rewards the wealthy, or the elitist system of government.

It is the refocusing of social insecurities through the prism of a politicized racial divide that explains the power of the modern crime panic. That is why the fear of violent crime can be so disproportionate to any real problem, and why seemingly irrational scares can take hold of the suburban imagination so forcefully. The "carjacking" panic of the early 1990s is a classic example of this process.

The image of young Black criminals from the ghetto stealing the cars and threatening the children of suburbanites at gunpoint was perfectly designed to touch a raw nerve among many White Americans and provoke a racial response. Despite the fact that almost all carjacking takes place within the ghettos itself, and that there had been just two grim incidents of White shoppers being carjacked when the scare took off, the media and the authorities went out of their way to inflate the panic about "urban terrorism" spreading to the White suburbs, and to exploit the racially charged response in order to win support for another law-and-order crusade. In a typical example, the governor of New Jersey declared his determination to keep the ghetto "plague" at bay: "We haven't yet seen the epidemic plaguing other areas around the nation and we're not willing to. We intend to escalate our response to a full-scale assault on the problem."[4] That full-scale assault was to include getting the FBI to include carjacking "with gang activity and drug-related violence as crimes investigated by a 300-member arm of the agency formed in January with former foreign counter-intelligence agents.[5] By exploiting the carjacking panic to help them present "street terrorists" from the ghetto as the new Enemy of the American People, the U.S. elites were able to mobilize support for targeting young Black males in New York with former secret service agents, who had been made redundant by the end of the Cold War.

CRIME PANICS DO PAY

The crime scare has been promoted by politicians and the media as a major reason for middle-class America to retreat behind its security walls and leave the police to deal with the inner cities. Through these coded issues, race relations are increasingly being discussed in terms of Good and Evil. Entire inner-city communities are being criminalized and treated as a violent plague to be policed in military fashion. Through this approach, the dominant elites are reinforcing the racial divide in society—not in openly racist terms, but in the language of law and order. The elites have much to gain from this process.

How much easier it is for a president to appear authoritative by announcing a high-profile war against crime, rather than by trying to tackle the scourge of structural unemployment. How much more effective it is for an aspiring congressman to appeal to suburban voters by demanding a crackdown on carjacking or burglary, rather than by raising the desperate plight of the inner cities. And how much "sexier" it is for a newspaper or television news editor to lead with a story about crack epidemics and dramatic drive-by shootings, rather than to report on boring old stuff like poverty and discrimination.

But there is also a more profound political process at work. Through the racially loaded crime discussion, sections of the American elites are seeking to create what we might call a *new counterpoint to normalcy* for the post-Cold War era. The "Us-against-Them" ideology of the Cold War years gave the U.S. authorities a uniquely powerful political framework through which to mobilize support for the status quo and to draw a line between right and wrong in public life. In the culture of anti-communism, anything that strayed too far from the official lines could be branded as "un-American" and immediately discredited. The collapse of the Soviet Union and the end of the Cold War robbed the powers that be of that effective method of boosting their authority. Through coded racial issues, such as the crime panics of today, some are seeking to create an alternative Us-against-Them climate that can be utilized for reactionary political purposes. The criminal "underclass" is set up as a counterpoint to the normalcy of respectable Americans, as a threat against which decent people should unite (behind the authorities). It should be obvious to all who care to see that the divide which is really being deepened by the top-level promotion of this counterpoint is the division between the races.

In effect, through the panic about Black criminal males from the ghetto, some of the most powerful voices in the United

States are setting up some of the most powerless Americans as the cause of the country's major problem. This is a process that can have considerable political payoffs for the elites. It is also one for which Black people in the inner cities pay a very high price.

The atmosphere of suspicion and division created by the elite manipulation of the issue of race and crime was illustrated in dramatic fashion by the case of Susan Smith. In October 1994, this 23-year-old White woman from the small town of Union, South Carolina reported that a young Black man had ordered her out of her Mazda at gunpoint, then drove it away with her two baby sons—3-year old Michael and 14-month-old Alexander—still strapped in the back seat. The community was horrified, and desperate searches for the children were launched. Then, nine days later, Susan Smith admitted that she had, in fact, got out of her car and rolled it into the local lake, deliberately drowning her own children. The young Black man with the gun did not exist.

The Smith case evoked memories not only of old-time racist lynchings but of a 1989 incident in Boston. In that incident, a White man, Charles Stuart, had shot and killed his pregnant wife, Carol, in their car, and blamed the murder on a Black carjacker. And again, he was immediately believed; police launched stop and search sweeps through Black housing projects, and even charged a Black man with the murder, before Stuart's story was exposed and he killed himself.

When the truth about the 1994 Smith killings became known, the reaction from many Black people can be summed up in one phrase: "It is always the Black man." As one Black man told the press, "I guess she figured if she said a Black man did it people would believe her no matter what kind of story she came up with...As long as it's allegedly a Black man involved, America will fall for anything." A Black sociology lecturer thought that the case confirmed "the stereotypical view of

Black men in America, that they are other, that they are dangerous, that they should be imprisoned."[6]

This association between the Black man and violent crime is the key to the success of the crime panics for America's dominant elites. Through systematically promoting the counterpoint between the criminal Black "underclass" and respectable citizens, the authorities have ensured the creation of an atmosphere of racial hostility that reinforces conservative attitudes towards the need for firmer law and order and more social control. In this atmosphere, there is an automatic willingness among many White Americans to identify the Black male with violent crime, to believe that he must be capable of anything. That this outlook is the product of a politicized racial divide, rather than a real experience of crime, should be clear from the fact that Susan Smith's story could so readily be believed in a town like Union, where there is not very much crime.

Some of the benefits that the creation of such an association between Black males and crime can bring to the authorities was well illustrated during the Rodney King saga. Despite clear videotape evidence of the savage beating that they had handed out to Rodney King, four LAPD officers were initially acquitted of all charges by a jury that contained ten White people and no Blacks. (Two of the officers were later found guilty of lesser civil rights charges.)

Many stunned commentators asked, in the immediate aftermath of the trial, How was it possible that the jury could have ignored the evidence of their own eyes and found the four police officers not guilty? More perceptive commentators saw that the racial climate surrounding all law-and-order issues was more important than any specific piece of evidence in shaping the opinions of a jury drawn from the conservative suburb of Simi Valley. "That jury," said Henry Louis Gates, chair of Afro-American Studies at Harvard, "was more afraid of the potential of being mugged by some hypothetical Black male than it was of the abuse of the Constitution, of civil rights."[7] Others have since noted how, by drawing a stereotype of the violent, drug-crazed Black male, the attorneys defending the LAPD officers conducted their case in such a way as to put Rodney King, the victim, on trial. "The defense attorneys, in effect, played the so-called 'race card'"; argued LAPD officers, Oliver, Johnson, and Farrell: "they painted Mr. King as unpredictable, dangerous and uncontrollable."[8]

The Rodney King saga and its aftermath is a symbol of the virtual war that U.S. police forces, with the support of other governmental agencies, are waging against sections of the Black and minority communities in the inner city. Yet armed with the power of the racial crime panic, the American elites were able to twist this incident into a sign of the need for firmer policing to deal with Black crime. The authorities responsible for the tragedy were not only let off the hook but left with renewed authority to appeal to decent Americans to support the forces of law-and-order in a crackdown on the urban terrorists and barbarians.

A predisposition towards law-and-order solutions to issues concerning the Black poor has been instilled in majority American opinion from the top down. It is important to consider how this phenomenon has recently operated in practice—giving the ruling elites more scope to pursue policies of containment and control in the ghetto, and allowing them to shape the subsequent public debate about racial conflict in the ghetto.

A FEW BAD APPLES!

Nobody can seriously deny that the police forces of the United States use a lot of force to police the ghetto. The issue is, how much of this force is deployed as a measure of social control, and how much is a genuine response to the threat of

Black crime? Under the influence of the elite ideological tools outlined above, mainstream opinion today holds that the police are generally justified in using force against Black criminals. When it becomes clear that some police officers have gone further and have overstepped the mark, the typical response is to separate their specific actions from the general practice of the police force.

"A few bad apples don't spoil the whole bunch" is the principle with which U.S. public opinion approaches established cases of police brutality. Thus most commentators, who were initially very critical of the Rodney King beating and acquittal, framed their accusations very narrowly at the individual officers and jurors involved, rather than at the police and judicial system as a whole. Much was made of the fact that some of the police officers accused had long personal records of using force. Edwin Delattre, a Boston University ethics professor who has written a book on the use of force that is widely used as a police training manual, claimed that he had talked to hundreds of police officers around the country who were themselves enraged by what they saw on the videotape of Rodney King's ordeal: "They [the police] feel betrayed by the low standards of the police in Los Angeles. There is indignation and resentment; they believe the four cops in LA should have been convicted. Police all over the country are appalled that those police used force in such a contemptible way."[9]

But the beating of Rodney King did not really "betray" the impartial standards of the LAPD or other American police forces. There was only one exceptional thing about the incident—the fact that a civilian named George Holiday and his Handicam were on hand to record it for television and posterity. In every other respect, the beating of Rodney King could be seen as a pretty typical example of how America polices the Black communities of its inner cities. It is a sign of the success of the Black crime panic for the elites, that they are able to brutalize and occupy entire inner-city communities on a systematic basis, while brushing off those incidents when they get caught as the work of a few "bad apples."

Look a little more closely at what provoked unrest in America's cities over the past 25 years, and a pattern begins to emerge. Somewhere within the complex causes of various riots, the immediate spark was provided by an example of police harassment or violence. In the eyes of many Black and (more recently) Latino people, who have to put up with such treatment as a fact of everyday life, each of those incidents came to be seen as one case too many of their communities being pushed around by an unjust police force.

Rodney King was beaten senseless because he initially refused to stop for a police patrol car, which tried to pull him over for speeding. He had been drinking and, he later claimed in court, was afraid that speeding would be considered a violation of his parole. (King had recently been released from jail after serving a sentence for robbery.) For the crime of failing to stop his car, King was shot twice with a stun gun and hammered at least 56 times with batons before being arrested (the city attorney's office eventually dropped all charges against him).

Those commentators who suggested that what happened to Rodney King was an exception, the work of "bad apples," might look back to the events that sparked the Watts riot in Los Angeles over 25 years ago, in 1965. The circumstances involved a Black motorist accused of speeding, who appeared to have been drinking, and a number of policemen with clubs, who laid into Black bystanders and provoked a riot. This pattern of the "routine" policing of Black communities finally provoking a backlash against police racism has repeated itself time and again since Watts.

For instance, in Detroit in 1967, a routine police raid on a "blind pig" (an after-hours drinking joint) got out of hand when the raiding officers called up heavy reinforcements and loaded 82 people into their cars. The result was the start of what has been described as the worst urban riot in American history. In

Miami in 1980, a Black motorcyclist, Arthur McDuffie, allegedly "popped a wheelie" and "gave the finger" to a police patrol car. For this heinous crime, McDuffie was soon being pursued by police officers, and ended up on the sidewalk with his head split open and his brain swelling uncontrollably. He died four days later. It was not McDuffie's death that caused the riot in Miami, however; it was the announcement, in May 1980, that the police officers involved had all been acquitted. There was another riot in Miami in January 1989, and the immediate causes fit the same pattern. This time it was sparked off by the police shooting another Black motorcyclist who was riding away from them.[8] More recently still, in 1992, the acquittal of police who beat to death an alleged Latino drug dealer caused another riot in Miami.

Policing is the frontline of the racial divide in modern America. A single act of police brutality can provoke such a backlash, not just because of the incident itself, but because it becomes an instantaneous symbol of the way in which the authorities treat Black and other minority communities in the inner cities. Looking at the record of police violence against minority communities, the surprising thing is not that there have been riots but that there have been so few serious outbreaks of public disorder. If there was a riot every time the police shot a Black man without good cause, much of America would have burned to the ground long ago. Between 1976 and 1987 (the latest period for which figures are available), around 1,800 Blacks and 3,000 Whites were killed by law enforcement officers in the United States. In other words, given the proportion of the population which they make up, Black Americans have a three-times-greater chance than Whites of being shot dead by a policeman.[10] These shootings are only the bloody tip of an iceberg of repression that the U.S. authorities have imposed and legitimized in the ghetto, under cover of the panic about Black crime threatening American civilization.

"PROACTIVE" REPRESSION

The Los Angeles Police Department offers something of a model of the use of crime panics for the purposes of social control in the desperate communities of the inner city. The modern LAPD was created in the 1950s by Chief William Parker, the policing equivalent of that other leading liberal of the time, J. Edgar Hoover.

An ex-Marine, Parker set out to turn the Los Angeles Police Department into an elite Marine Corps of American policing, a "thin blue line" protecting civilization. The method with which the LAPD would control crime among that population was to be known as "proactive policing."

In theory, the idea behind proactive policing is to deter crime in the first place, instead of having to solve it afterwards. Treating crime as a disease, the proactive police force seeks to operate on the accepted medical principle that prevention is always better than cure. In practice, however, the proactive policing of the Los Angeles Police Department has more often looked like a case of what some sports fans might recognize as the tactic of "getting your retaliation in first."

One of the most important aspects of proactive policing has been the use of so-called criminal profiles. This is a system designed to identify what sort of people belong in certain parts of the city at certain times, and what sort of people do not. After Parker's appointment, the racial composition of Los Angeles began to change, as Whites moved out to the suburbs and more and more of the inner city became populated by Black and Latino people. The LAPD's response was to make race the most important factor in deciding a criminal profile. Blacks from the inner city were expected to stay there; any Black male spotted in a White residential area was likely to be moved along back to "where he belongs," or even arrested for the crime of walking the wrong streets. The plush new shopping malls of modern downtown Los Angeles operate a similar informal system of segregation. There are no signs up (as yet) saying "Black and Latino youths keep out," but the LAPD-inspired private police forces and surveillance cameras make the message loud and clear.

The impact of this kind of racial-criminal profiling has been considerable over the past four decades. In practical terms it has meant that the segregation of Los Angeles has not only been encouraged and endorsed by the business and political elites, but has been enforced at the highest levels of the forces of law-and-order. It has meant the construction of an invisible wall, effectively caging the Black and Latino poor within their ghetto communities. In terms of public perceptions of the crime problem, the impact has been equally dramatic. Through the LAPD's use of racially biased criminal profiles, official sanction has been given to the notion that Blacks are all potential criminals who cannot be trusted in respectable White areas of the city and its suburbs. The White public's widespread acceptance of that official line has given the authorities a free hand to impose even more systematic measures of exclusion and control on the marginalized communities of the inner cities.

The most famous chiefs of the Los Angeles police over the past 40 years have made little secret of their own racial feelings. Chief Parker's ethos on the question of race was clear and unambiguous, and he spelled it out for all to hear when racial tensions in Los Angeles exploded in the Watts riots of 1965. The LAPD and the National Guard killed more than 30 Blacks. Parker's department declared each and every killing to be a "justifiable homicide," and the Chief himself denounced the unrest as the work of a handful of "riff-raff," of a few "monkeys in a zoo." After the riot, Chief Parker went on television to issue an apocalyptic warning to the White population of Los Angeles: "It is estimated that by 1970, 45 percent of the metropolitan area of Los Angeles will be Negro. If you want any protection for your home and family...you're going to have to get in and support a strong police department. If you don't, come 1970, God help you."[11]

Parker's best-known successor was his onetime driver and lifelong admirer, Daryl Gates, who became Chief of Police in Los Angeles in 1978. The Daryl Gates school of racial policing was clearly defined during the controversy about the LAPD's use of a strangling "chokehold" to restrain young Black men. In 1982, there was an outcry after 15 people had died through being locked in a police chokehold. Gates offered the explanation that this was due to the racial anatomy of the victims, rather than any racist violence by the police. "We may be finding that in some Blacks when [the chokehold] is applied the veins or arteries do not open up as fast as they do on normal people."[12]

These open expressions of prejudice by Parker and Gates have led some commentators to propose a kind of "big bad apple" theory of police repression, i.e., to suggest that the despicable record of the LAPD in policing the Black inner cities from the fifties to the nineties has been largely a product of the individual bigotry of the chiefs of police. But that seriously underestimates both the extent and the racially defined patterns of repression. Parker and Gates were simply crude exponents of the system of racial policing that, under them and every other chief, has been institutionalized in every major American city.

In Los Angeles, the officially endorsed scares about Black crime and racial violence became the pretext for empowering the police force on an unprecedented scale. After the Watts riots, the process of para-militarization gathered pace within the Los Angeles Police Department. Parker's vision of an elite, self-contained, and hi-tech police force had always eschewed such traditional notions of policing as the neighborhood patrol. That trend towards militarizing the LAPD really took off after the Watts riots.

Police helicopters were introduced as the central means of surveillance in the ghettos, a tactic ideally suited to a "horizontal city" such as Los Angeles. More recently, under the "Astro" program, the LAPD has kept up a 19-hour-a-day vigil over "high crime" (that is, Black and Hispanic) areas, using Aerospatiele choppers with infra-red night-eyes and super-powerful "Nightsun" spotlights (which, as camcorder operator William Halliday can testify, live up to their name). The LAPD, the police force that first pioneered the use of SWAT teams, also greatly increased its firepower and its capacity to blow away anybody, like the Black Panther Party, who attempted to stand up to the force. Chief Parker's experiments with both paramilitary helicopters and shoot-to-kill squads are good examples of how the alleged "bad apple" of the LAPD has often really been the trend-setter in repressive methods which other forces have been quick to copy.

The Los Angeles Police Department has pursued its policy of proactively policing minority communities with an increasingly hi-tech infrastructure of repression. The divisive siege mentality emanating from the very top of the LAPD has been built into the structure of the city itself. The police department has worked with city planners to design the new downtown shopping-, residential-, and financial-sector developments as a kind of fortress, protected from Black and Latino hordes outside by private-police footpatrols, which are backed by the LAPD's computerized, helicopter-led system of surveillance and arrest. There are powerful lobbyists now pushing for this system to be supplemented by a police satellite over Los Angeles.

For Mike Davis, who has extensively documented this trend towards "Robocop" methods and LAPD-supervised urban redevelopment, the prospect of a police version of Star Wars to add to all the other technology sums up what he sees as "the historical world view and quixotic quest of the postwar LAPD":

"Good citizens, off the streets, enclaved in their high-security private consumption spheres; bad citizens, on the streets (and therefore not engaged in legitimate business), caught in the terrible, Jehovan scrutiny of the LAPD's space program."[13]

No doubt it is possible for a few middle-class Blacks to become good citizens, and for poor Whites to cross the line in the other direction; but in the electronic eye of the Los Angeles Police Department, the basic border between good and bad is pretty clearly a racial one.

The LAPD doctrine of proactive policing was responsible for the terrible beating handed out to Rodney King in March 1991, and the experience of such systematic police violence and harassment was also responsible for the fury with which many people in Los Angeles reacted to the acquittal of the four officers. And proactive policing made itself felt during the Los Angeles riots themselves. The television coverage of the 1992 violence tended to focus on images of Blacks attacking White motorists, and it would have been easy to gain the impression that the 58 killed in the disturbances were all out-of-town truckers. The facts are, however, that the majority of those killed were young Black males; that more than half of them were killed by the Los Angeles Police Department and the National Guardsmen; and that there was not one LAPD fatality. And when the city was calm again, the government sent in the FBI and the crack team of federal marshals who had captured Manuel Noriega in Panama to back up the LAPD's proactive attempts to track down the alleged gang instigators of the riot.

The personalities of Chiefs Parker and Gates did not cause racism in the LAPD; they merely reflected the ethos of racial policing and social control institutionalized in the police and legal system. Barely two months after the Los Angeles riots, Daryl Gates was succeeded as chief of the LAPD by Willie Williams, a Black man. In the week that he took over, an LAPD officer shot dead an unarmed 36-year-old Black truck driver at the Crenshaw-Florence intersection, in the heart of the district where the riots erupted. The victim's father had been shot dead by police in 1985, during Chief Gates's heyday. The killing of Mr. Daniels Jr., by the same force could be said to give a fair idea of just how different things were going to be in South Central Los Angeles under the new Black police chief.

This is the true face of policing in Los Angeles and the other major cites of modern America. It is a system designed to control and keep in place those whom society is incapable of integrating and treating as equals. Getting rid of one bigot like Daryl Gates, and replacing him with a Black chief of police, is not going to fundamentally alter things. Those who believed that it might do so must have been swiftly disillusioned. Such cosmetic changes in the structure of the police department of Los Angeles or any other American city can make no significant difference, because the problem of the policing of non-Anglo communities goes much deeper. It strikes at the very heart of a society in which discrimination is still institutionalized from the top down, and where a primary role of the police is to patrol the racial divide and contain the Black communities of the inner city.

Yet the focus of public debate refuses to remain for more than a moment on the problem that the police pose to minorities, before switching back to talk about the problems that the police face in controlling Black and Latino ghettos. The issue of Black crime dominates public and political discourse, its images and stereotypes providing a ready-made excuse for whatever measures the police and courts choose to take.

The defenders of proactive policing—some of them, as we shall see later, within the Black community itself—will say that the hi-tech repressive policing of the 1980s and 1990s is never simply about racism. It is, they claim, about dealing with the inner-city problems of drugs and crime and gangs in places like New York or Los Angeles. These problems are undeniably real and very serious, and they touch the lives of many people. Indeed, by claiming that their aim is to clean up the neighborhood and kick out the pushers and the gang-bangers, the police have often been able to win grudging acceptance from people in the cities who see the drug trade and the violence it breeds as the most pressing problem facing their families and their communities.

But the repressive activities of the police and legal system are not, and could not be, designed to deal with the deep-rooted social problems that give rise to violence in the inner cities. Instead, the issues of drugs and gangs and guns have been used as a convenient pretext for criminalizing the Black and Latino communities to which the American system can offer no future, and thus enabling the authorities to keep the dispossessed under control by militarizing everyday life in large areas of the modern American city. A brief look at what is really behind the Reagan/Bush "war on drugs" and Clinton's crusade for gun control bears this out.

WHO'S LOSING THE "WAR ON DRUGS"?

It should not come as a surprise to anyone that there is a drug problem in America's inner-cities. Such problems are the inevitable product of the degraded and marginalized status to which the ghetto communities of the United States are condemned. Using heavy drugs is often an attempt to escape, at least momentarily, from the desperate circumstances of poverty and deprivation in which many in those communities are forced to live. The selling of drugs, meanwhile, and the violence that accompanies it, has flourished in conditions where the ghetto's economic decay and isolation provide few conventional outlets for entrepreneurial flair to flourish.

The "war on drugs," launched under the presidencies of Ronald Reagan and George Bush, was not, however, designed to tackle the social causes of the drug problem. Look at any of the media interviews with Black or Latino youth in which they are asked what is behind the drug/gang culture. You will see that almost all of them say there can be no end to widespread drug dealing and abuse in the ghetto unless an alternative economy is created, one that can provide jobs and decent living standards for people in their communities—and not just for the small elite of the new Black middle classes. The federal, state, and city authorities have, however, made only the most token of efforts to address the social crisis that is behind the drug issue. Instead, they have devoted immense resources to treating drugs simply as a law-and-order issue—or, as it is often called, a war, "another Vietnam."

The "war on drugs" that was launched from the Republican White House and has been fought by every institution of official America has not been about dealing with the social causes of the drug problem. It has been the pretext for a highly militarized policing operation designed to contain and control the disenfranchised communities of the inner cities. As such, the bitter irony is that the "war on drugs" has worked to maintain precisely those conditions of marginalization and degradation that produced the drug problem on such a scale in the first place.

There is a long-standing connection between the issues of drugs and race in American politics. Official anti-drug drives have often been thinly disguised racist campaigns to impose tighter controls over minority communities that the authorities sought to link with drugs—the opium-smoking "heathen Chinese," or the dope-smoking "beet peons" from Mexico, or the hopped-up "cocainized Negroes" of the Deep South.

The war on drugs of the eighties and nineties is in many ways the modern face of this old American tradition, a crusade designed to tighten state controls over Blacks and Latinos in the desolate inner cities whom America has pushed to the margins and robbed of all hope, and now has to contain.

By linking Black communities inextricably with drugs and violent crime, America's ruling elites have exploited public concern in order to justify more and more military-style policing in cities such as New York, Washington, and Los Angeles. An understanding of this process of manipulation provides a powerful riposte to those who have tried to minimize or to misrepresent the problem of police racism and violence. Nobody can claim that the "war on drugs" is the invention of individual officers in the Los Angeles Police Department. It has been promoted at every level of the U.S government and legal system, from the White House downwards. Yet this national war on drugs, with all of its presidential authority, is in practice little more than a rhetorical device used to legitimize the kind of paramilitary policing methods that Americans would more usually associate with a foreign police state.

That Washington is fully behind the repression associated with the "war on drugs" was never clearer than in April 1989, when then First Lady Nancy Reagan actually accompanied the LAPD on a drug raid in South Central Los Angeles. Admittedly, she did stay outside in a luxury motor home with "THE ESTABLISHMENT" painted on it, eating lunch with Chief of Police Daryl Gates, until the SWAT team had secured the alleged "rock house." The first lady of the United States then entered the bungalow while 14 "narco-terrorists" still lay handcuffed on the floor. She announced to the assembled press corps that, "These people in here are beyond the point of teaching or rehabilitating."[14] The thoughts of those people in there regarding this remarkable spectacle are unrecorded.

That particular raid was obviously very unusual, but it also said a lot about the general character of the American states' "war on drugs." It was a high-profile publicity stunt that scored some good points for the Republican administration, gave Chief Gates a touch of glamour, and showed off the LAPD's paramilitary methods. As such, the Nancy Reagan raid was a success for all involved in it. It did nothing whatsoever to address the causes or the consequences of the drug problem in Los Angeles. But then, it was never intended to. The "war on drugs" has really been a war on the ghetto communities, a war of occupation in the inner cities. The top-level campaign to associate drugs with Blacks has served to excuse repression on a massive and unprecedented scale in the public mind.

In Los Angeles, the paramilitary occupation of the inner-city ghettos was carried out under Operation HAMMER, a series of high-profile raids using the new powers granted to the LAPD under STEP—the Street Terrorism Enforcement and Prevention Act of 1988, which made gang membership itself a criminal offense for the first time. And in the hands of the American policing and legal system, being a gang member simply meant being Black or Latino.

In HAMMER's initial mass raids on inner-city Los Angeles, the police hauled more Black youth off to jail than at any time since the Watts riots of two decades before. Arresting (and sometimes shooting at) those suspected of belonging to gangs meant in practice pulling in anybody seen wearing, say, red shoelaces, or giving each other a high-fives handshake. Most HAMMER arrests had nothing to do with drugs, but were more likely to be for drinking or for violating the police-imposed curfews in areas subject to LAPD occupation. In other words, hundreds of young Blacks and Latinos were arrested for committing "offenses" that would not have been considered illegal at all in an "Anglo" area of the city.

The most notorious HAMMER raid took place in August 1988, in the Dalton Street area of South Central LA. Police ran riot, beating up many residents, wrecking apartments, and even scrawling "LAPD Rules" alongside the "Crips" and "Bloods" gang graffiti on the walls. Thirty-two people were arrested and abused in custody; just two were eventually charged with minor drug offenses. When it was all over, the Red Cross offered Dalton Street disaster assistance—something usually associated with natural catastrophes in the third world.

The poor results and bad publicity associated with HAMMER prompted LAPD Chief Gates to change tactics—not by withdrawing his army of occupation, but by digging it in on a more permanent basis. He created "Narcotic Enforcement

Zones," America's first domestic experience of Vietnam-style strategic hamlets. These areas are closed to all but residents, and can be entered or left only through police barricades. Their establishment marked a new era of proactive policing. In October 1989, the LAPD sealed off 30 blocks with checkpoints in "Operation Cul-de-Sac." The next month, just as the Berlin Wall was coming down in Europe, Los Angeles's own version of the wall was extended into the barrio and down Central Avenue in South Central. The racial divide in Los Angeles had now become a physical one, controlled by the thin blue line.

Meanwhile, the LA legal authorities were imposing new laws that pressed landlords to evict the families of those ARRESTED on drug-related charges, before they had even been tried or convicted. All of these police and judicial measures have been accompanied by a non-stop barrage of propaganda against the "street terrorism" of 13-year-old Blacks and Latinos in South Central Los Angeles, a campaign using the most emotive language of our age to justify fighting a war against America's own people on its own streets.

From the invention of special offenses for Black and Latino youth to the unequal treatment handed out by the courts, the racial bias of the "war on drugs" is clear enough. How else would you explain the huge disparity, noted by the *Los Angeles Times*, between the sentences handed out to Black youths found guilty of carrying small amounts of "crack" cocaine and those given to Whites caught with the "designer drug," cocaine powder?

"Under new federal statutes, defendants convicted of selling 5 grams or more of crack cocaine, worth perhaps $125, receive a mandatory minimum of five years in prison. However, it takes 500 grams of the powered drug, nearly $50,000 worth of "yuppie" cocaine, to receive an equivalent sentence. Consequently, someone caught in a drug bust with a relatively small amount of cocaine can receive a sentence that is two to three years longer than a person convicted of selling nearly 100 times that amount."[15]

No doubt some would say that this disparity in sentencing policy reflects the more addictive and dangerous character of "crack" cocaine. Those who have looked more closely at how the "war on drugs" is waged in a city such as Los Angeles might draw a different conclusion.

"More Americans are in federal prison for drug crimes than were in federal prison for all crimes when Ronald Reagan took office [in January, 1981]...And half the Americans in prison today are Black, even though only about one-eighth of the population is. The United States, in fact, has a rate of Black male incarceration five times that of South Africa. More American Black men are in prison than are in college. The Justice Department estimates that by 1995, more than two-thirds of all convicts will be inside for drugs. This isn't a war on drugs; its a jihad against people who use them."[16]

The above report by Dan Baum contains many other frightening facts about what he calls "the drug war on civil liberties": the way in which the federalizing of drug crimes has created a maximum five-year sentence for a first offense of possessing marijuana; the fact that casual users of drugs have not only been jailed for possession but also ejected from public housing, deprived of their driver's licenses and had student loans or welfare payments cut off; and the way that, under the banner of the war on drugs, the Supreme Court has eroded the protections against police excess enshrined in the Fourth, Fifth, Sixth, Eighth and Fourteenth Amendments to the American Constitution.

In effect, anything becomes permissible once the magic word "drugs" is whispered. The association of drugs with race by the political and other elites has ensured that the draconian "war on drugs" can be pursued with so little public criticism.

The fact that the Republican administrations were not interested in tackling the social crisis behind the drug problem in the inner cities became clearer still after Bush launched the "Weed and Seed" strategy in 1991. Twenty cities, including Los Angeles, Chicago, Philadelphia, and Seattle, were quickly involved in this federal scheme, and more have been signed up since. The theory behind Weed and Seed is as follows: first, federal agents and local law enforcement agencies "weed" the criminals out of the inner cities; then, these cleaned-up areas are "seeded" with federal grants. In practice, however, the campaign is heavy on the weeding and thin on the seeding. Weed and Seed is another containment strategy disguised as a program of public investment.

In 1992, the Weed and Seed program, run by the Justice Department, was funded to the tune of $500 million. But just $13.5 million of that money was new funds. The rest was previously allocated social-service money, which the Justice Department simply took away from the Department of Housing and Urban Development, the Department of Health and Human Services, and other government departments. In effect, under the banner of Weed and Seed, the Justice Department has integrated inner-city social services into an all-round strategy for policing impoverished communities. It has been suggested that this strategy "prefigures the ultimate absorption of the welfare state by the police state."[17]

The major "social benefits" that various cities have gained from being involved in the Weed and Seed program include, not better welfare and social investment or employment programs, but federal agents scouring the streets, mobile police stations, big paramilitary sweeps, and aerial and video surveillance courtesy of the National Guard and the Bureau of Alcohol, Tobacco, and Firearms. Added to this are the militarized housing projects, with their metal detectors and security guards on every building, where people have to show ID to enter their own homes.

And then there is perhaps the most sinister element of Weed and Seed—the FAST track prosecution conveyor belt

(Federal Alternatives to State Trial). This program streamlines the system to give long prison sentences even to first-time offenders who are arrested in target areas. Possession of a few grams of crack in a Weed and Seed target area can get someone with a clean record a quick route to five years in jail. According to the attorney general's 1992 Weed and Seed report to Congress, the federal FAST track conviction program boasts a terrifying 99 percent conviction rate. Thus the Weed and Seed program has been predicated on treating Black youth, no longer even as street terrorists, but as weeds to be pulled out and discarded on a heap. Getting away with such an overtly repressive strategy of containment and control in the inner cities is the harvest that the authorities have reaped from the carefully planted notion that dealing with the drug problem is really the problem of dealing with the Black and Latino poor in the ghetto.

CLINTON'S CRUSADE

After Bill Clinton's election in 1992, his Democratic administration showed no signs of abandoning the legal and policing assault on the inner cities. Instead, in its attempt to consolidate support in the suburbs, the Clinton administration has tried to take up the Republican law-and-order mantle and to pursue the crusade against inner-city youth. The effect has been to reinforce all of the elite notions about the criminal tendencies of Black men from the inner city.

The character of Clinton's anti-crime program became clear in the November 1993 bill that provided $8.9 billion for 100,000 more cops and extended the death penalty to 52 new offenses, including killing a government poultry inspector. The president emphasized the centrality of the "war on crime" again in his January 1994 State of the Union address. Of course, the Clinton administration has not promoted its anti-crime initia-

tives in racial terms. It talks about tackling the problems associated with drugs and guns. But crack the code, and we can see
that the present U.S. government is propounding a message
that is just as racially loaded as the campaigns associated with
Reagan or Bush. More Black and liberal leaders may have been
brought on board; but the target of the campaign remains the
Black and Latino "underclass" of the inner cities.

It is possible to see this strategy by looking at the real
meaning of Clinton's 1993-94 campaign to introduce new gun
controls. The Brady Bill, part of Clinton's anti-crime package,
was the first federal gun legislation for 25 years. It established
a five-day waiting period for buying handguns. Clinton also
signed two presidential directives that suspended the importa-
tion of "assault pistols" and started a review of the rules gov-
erning gun dealerships.

Campaigning for such gun control may seem like a laudable liberal aim. After all, a total of 37,155 Americans died from
gunshot wounds in 1990.[18] There are an estimated 200 million
guns in circulation in the United States today, 40 million of
which are easily concealed hand guns. The horrifying stories of
drive-by shootings on the street or drug-related gang shoot-
outs in the schoolyard have convinced many people that strin-
gent gun controls are the only solution. There is a growing sense
that Americans have lost control over their own neighborhoods,
their own children.

But behind these harrowing statistics, the campaign for
gun control is about something else entirely. It is not a campaign
against guns as such. It is all a question of WHOSE FINGER IS
ON THE TRIGGER. The message is that while respectable
Americans can be trusted with guns, the criminally inclined
Black communities of the ghetto cannot.

Few gun control enthusiasts campaign to have the police
disarmed, despite the fact that their guns produce the largest
percentage of "justifiable homicides," making up around a
third of total gun homicides. Indeed, big-city police forces have

been some of the most ardent supporters of more restrictions. Clearly, the campaign for gun control is not primarily about saving lives. It is about allowing the authorities to decide who can and cannot be trusted. And, as ever, the unspoken issue of race underpins much of the discussion.

The call for gun control in the United States began about a hundred years ago, as part of the anxiety about the sprawling immigrant communities in American cities. Most local restrictions, such as the 1911 Sullivan Law in New York City, were passed between 1890 and 1917, the high point of immigration from eastern and southern Europe. As one writer observes, those calling for gun control back then were certainly not liberals: "In the 19th and early 20th century, gun-control laws were often targeted at Blacks in the South and foreign-born in the North.[19]

In the sixties, the lobby for gun controls reflected anxieties about America's increasingly Black inner cities. In 1968, the Gun Control Act was passed, ostensibly in response to the assassinations of Robert Kennedy and Martin Luther King. But the Act was really in response to three consecutive summers of Black rioting in America's inner cities. Hence, the main tenet of the Act was the restriction of cheap, imported pistols such as the "Saturday Night Special," the affordable guns of the Black ghetto.

The new developments in the debate about gun control reflect intensifying hostility toward the inner cities and their Black and Latino residents, rather than anything to do with the weapons themselves. For example, "assault" weapons are the current subject of lurid magazine stories. "These weapons have got to go," exclaimed the then chief of the Los Angeles Police Department, Daryl Gates, summoning up fears of gang killings before a Senate panel in 1992. Yet at the same time, the LAPD's own South Bureau homicide unit's investigations revealed that of all fatal shootings in Los Angeles between 1990 and 1991, less than 2 percent involved assault weapons.[20]

The real reason for the selective assault on assault rifles is because of what, or rather who, these guns symbolized. As Bill Clinton put it in a 1993 press release, they are "the weapon of choice for drug dealers, street gang members, and other violent criminals." Here Clinton was using the well-known code with which racial buttons are pressed in American politics. "Drug-dealer" and "gang-member" are established in the public mind as euphemisms for Black and Latino inner-city dwellers. Now "assault weapon" has been added to the list of racial buzwords.

The hysteria about assault rifles is given an added twist today with the fears of gangs spreading out of the inner cities to the White suburbs. A *Time Magazine* cover story notes the danger: "Not long ago, many Americans dismissed the slaughter as an inner-city problem. But now the crackle of gunfire echoes from the poor urban neighborhoods to the suburbs of the heartland."[21] The "crackle of gunfire [which] echoes from the poor urban neighborhoods" has now become the focus of fears that American society is out of control. Tales of shooting sprees in shopping malls, movie theaters, and McDonald's restaurants frighten Middle Americans into barricading themselves against invasion by a growing "underclass" with an assault weapon in one hand and a welfare check in the other.

Unfortunately, state gun controls are unlikely to save any lives. But the message behind the gun-control campaign is likely to strengthen the consensus against Black and Latino inner-city communities. It plays upon fears of the gun-toting ghetto communities threatening the respectable suburbs. The endpoint is that the authorities and the police reinforce their right to use violence and their control over the lives of Black people in the inner cities. That is the ultimate consequence of the racially loaded anti-crime crusade in America. It is not about solving the problems of society. It is about criminalizing sections of that society, and militarizing the methods that can be used to contain them, and exploiting public fears to consolidate a conservative climate of support for the authorities in their war against the criminal "underclass."

At the time when Clinton's anti-crime package was passing through Congress, a White House aide made an amazing confession. "We don't know what causes crime," he admitted. "We have very little idea what deters it."[22] In which case, the multi-billion dollar anti-crime crusade clearly has little to do with its declared aims. It is a politically inspired attempt to prey on people's insecurities, seeking to reunite suburban America behind the political and legal elites against the stereotype of the assault-weapon-wielding, coked-up Black criminal.

5. THE INVENTION OF THE "UNDERCLASS"

The sociological category of "the underclass" has moved from obscurity to center field in social policy debates over recent years. But the high-level discussion about the problem of the "underclass" should not be taken at face value. In many ways, the "underclass" debate itself can be seen as the nub of the problem, a theme that pulls together all of the dangerous trends in the race discourse which the analysis presented here has identified.

The "underclass" debate captures the essence of the fashion for inverting reality or turning the truth on its head in the discourse about race relations and racism in the United States. First, the conservative emphasis upon the crisis of the "underclass" is essentially an attempt to locate the roots of Black poverty and social problems within the ghetto itself. The conservative argument about the "underclass" denies the existence of contemporary institutionalized discrimination and focuses instead on cultural and behavioral factors among the Black poor themselves in searching for an explanation for inequality. In this sense, the emergence of the "underclass" as an important subject of public debate symbolizes what has been identified elsewhere as a change in "the dominant mode of expression of prejudice and discrimination,"[1] which has shifted away from the old emphasis on the biological inferiority of the Black race and towards an explanation of inequality based on cultural differences. As we noted in our analysis of the different reactions to Charles Murray's earlier work on the "underclass" and his recent work on IQ and race, attempts to hold the Black urban "underclass" responsible for its own problems have become acceptable to liberals who reject old-fashioned biological theories of racial inferiority.

The second way in which the "underclass" debate typifies the attempt to turn the truth on its head is in the primary explanation it offers for racism among White Americans. The conservative critics of the "underclass" refute the idea that institutionalized discrimination is responsible for instilling a prejudiced outlook on the majority of the White population. Instead, they claim that what little White racism remains is attitudinal and largely a reaction against the immorality and criminal deviancy of the Black "underclass." In this view, the "White flight" to the suburbs was often motivated by the desire to escape from the culture of poverty, crime, and drugs that the Black "underclass" had made the dominant way of life in the American inner city.

From this perspective, it is not hard to see how the emphasis upon the existence of an "underclass" in contemporary social-policy discussion brings benefits to the ruling elites in American society. It allows them to shift responsibility for Black poverty from their own shoulders onto those of the poor themselves, and to generously admit that government's own failing has been in spending too much on welfare in the past—a "mistake" that both the Democratic and the Republican elites have made clear they are determined to put right with big cuts in the near future.

Elevating the problem of the "underclass" also serves a political function for the conservative elites. It provides a succinct counterpoint against which they can mobilize White sub-urban opinion. In this sense, the "underclass" debate is a pow-erful device with which the elites can focus the insecurities of many ordinary Americans onto racial, rather than social, issues. In emphasizing the involvement of the "underclass" in crime and urban decay, the spokesmen of the elites are drawing up a battleline between respectable American citizenry and the rab-ble—a line behind which they hope to consolidate a core of conservative support.

There is also, however, a broader message being transmit-ted through the high-profile "underclass" debate today. If the conservative assault upon the "underclass" were only about victimizing the Black poor, it would be objectionable enough. But there is even more at stake than the future of the inner-city communities. The moral crusade against the Black "underclass" is also an attempt to find a scapegoat for the failures of the entire American system. It is about undermining liberal criticisms of the way society as a whole is managed by the authorities.

The conservatives have not devoted so much time and effort to their assault on the "underclass" simply out of some irrational hatred for poor Blacks. They have done so in order to underpin their defense of the broader status quo in American society. Today's influential theories of the "underclass" have in effect become an all-purpose excuse for the failures and short-comings of the American economic and political system over the past three decades, much of which time has been spent struggling with economic recessions and political crises.

In condemning the Black urban "underclass" and its "cul-ture of poverty," the conservative thinkers are giving a lecture of wider significance to liberal opinionmakers. "See," the new racial thinkers are saying, "you have tried to do everything possible for these people in the past 30 years. You have had the War on Poverty, the Great Society, positive discrimination, af-firmative action, bussing, scholarships, and innumerable other publicly funded projects to support them. Yet at the end of all that, they are still stuck in the ghettos, up to their eyes in guns and drugs and fatherless babies."

"And that," continue the conservative ideologues, "can only prove that you cannot change things for the better through meddling welfare policies or throwing public money at the problem. Individuals will always find their own place in the natural order of things. Those without the moral fiber to take advantage of opportunities will sink to the bottom. The experience of the 'underclass' proves that giving them hand-outs from the taxpayer only makes their behavior and attitudes even worse."

This is the central message of the entire "underclass" debate—that you cannot solve the problem of poverty or deprivation by trying to change the way society is run through challenging the existing power structures.

By emphasizing the importance of moral and behavioral qualities, rather than social and economic inequalities, the "underclass" debate puts the responsibility firmly on the shoulders of the individual. Conservatives claim that America is a free and democratic society and that the best individuals will rise to the top, which is the reason that they are happy to sing the praises of the handful of middle-class Blacks who do make progress. The flipside of this argument is that if the Black poor are stuck at the bottom, it must be their own fault, a consequence of their "underclass" behavior, aided and abetted by liberal do-gooders. The structures of American society have nothing to do with it.

This argument has important and highly dangerous implications, not just for the Black poor, but for anybody concerned with social change and social justice. Economic failures and social malaise are explained away, not as a consequence of an elitist and socially inefficient system, but as the consequence of human attributes, as symbolized by the long-term experience of the Black urban poor.

If that were true, it would cease to be possible to argue for improving things by altering the way in which society is managed at the top. Instead, all we could hope for would be to try to change the behavior of the individuals at the bottom, presumably through a combination of persuasion and coercion. Thus conservative thinkers propose that policymakers should tackle the "underclass" problem by encouraging enterprise, family values, and a break in the cycle of dependency with a combination of moral lectures and welfare cuts. As for the immoral elements who refuse to heed these efforts, the logic of the "underclass" debate is that nothing can be done except to contain them through firmer policing measures of social control in the ghetto.

It is a grim vision of the future of the United States and western society. Yet it is one that serves the interests of the elites well in the current era. At a time of political crisis and economic stagnation, when these ruling elites can offer no positive vision of where society is heading, the theory of the Black "underclass" is perfectly tailored to their needs. It provides them with both a scapegoat for the social malaise and a focus against which to rally their forces.

To establish that the "underclass" debate is a useful one for the authorities to promote is not enough, however. To say that it can be manipulated by the elites is not the same as proving that it is an invention. What if the theory of the "underclass" and Black poverty is true? After all, its essence is now accepted by all shades of political opinion within the framework of the emerging post-liberal consensus. It is important, therefore, to take apart the influential arguments about the "underclass," in order that we might expose them as political and ideological constructions of the conservative elites, and so unearth their underlying motive of defending the status quo at the expense of the Black poor. Let us consider the case that is most often presented against the Black urban "underclass" in a little more detail.

DEFINING THE PROBLEM

In today's public discussions, prominence is given to the concept of the "underclass" and how to deal with it by conservatives and liberals alike. But exactly who or what do they mean by "underclass?"

The conservative definitions of what constitutes and characterizes this section of American society tend to be uncompromising and direct. The introductory article to an important survey of the subject in the journal *Public Interest* put it with characteristic vigor: "Violent crime, drug abuse, teen pregnancy, illiteracy, joblessness—these are some of the hallmarks of what has come to be called 'the underclass.'[2] Although the author did not say so explicitly, that article was also listing the characteristics that have shaped the "underclass" in what many conservatives would consider their order of importance: crime, drugs, teen pregnancy, and illiteracy at the top, with unemployment as something of an afterthought.

This kind of attack upon the "underclass" is part of a consistent political discourse on the U.S. Right. One of the most striking features of the debate, however, is the extent to which the concept of the underclass has been accepted and even embraced by many liberal commentators and by prominent Black spokespersons. A leading analyst of the issue offers this explanation of why the category "underclass" (with the emphasis on "under") appeals both to those who want to depict the Black Americans of the inner cities as downtrodden victims as well as to those who want to suggest that these people are in fact the guilty ones: "'Under' suggests the lowly, passive, and submissive, yet at the same time the disreputable, dangerous, disruptive, dark, evil, and even hellish."[3]

Whether or not other commentators see things in such melodramatic terms, it is certainly the case that the notion of a Black underclass has been accepted by all sides of the debate in the United States today. The existence and problematic character of such an underclass is now acknowledged and repeated, without serious critical thought, as a given fact of life in the United States.

It is my contention that the "Black underclass" is not a factual description of a section of American society at all. Instead, I would argue that the concept of the "Black underclass" is a political construction, created by conservatives for their own purpose. And if that is true, then the "Black underclass" is a concept with dangerous implications. It means that any discussion that begins—as all of today's major social policymakers' debates do—by accepting the existence of an underclass can ultimately benefit only those who want to blame Black people for the problems of American society.

The constant use of the very term "underclass" by rightwing commentators should at least set the alarm bells ringing. After all, most conservatives normally devote all of their energies to denying the relevance of class distinctions in the egalitarian and supposedly "classless" society of the United States. So why is it that they suddenly become so keen to stress the existence and importance of an underCLASS when it comes to explaining the predicament facing Blacks in the inner city? Instead of accepting the terms of discussion as laid down by the conservatives, we must subject the whole debate about the underclass to a rather more critical overview.

WHAT'S NEW?

Much of the discussion and disagreement about the Black underclass among academics and experts centers on why this group emerged to such prominence in the inner cities of America in recent years. There are minute investigations of income levels within deprived communities in an attempt to discover whether or not working-class people have become qualitatively poorer of late, whether more of them have somehow been tipped into the underclass, or whether instead we have witnessed the worsening status of a relatively small group of "underclass people" within a context of general improvement in living standards. The exchanges between Charles Murray and Christopher Jencks, over whether the growth of transfer payments have impoverished the poor rather than enriching them, are perhaps the most prominent example of this statistically based debate.[4]

Liberal analysts will often argue that the worsening economic position of the inner-city communities over the past 10 or 20 years has given rise to more of the characteristics that are usually defined as those of the underclass. Conservative commentators, on the other hand, will usually insist that the overall economic standing of Black communities and many other groups in the inner city has improved somewhat in modern times, but that the "hard-core" of the underclass has proved resistant to all attempts to improve its circumstances. Instead, say these conservatives, that core group has sunk deeper into the mire of the ghetto; and consequently it must be the strengthening of anti-social attitudes among these people that accounts for the new prominence that the problem of the underclass has acquired in current debates between social policymakers.

The debates about whether the underclass has been growing or shrinking, or whether the inner cities have experienced an absolute or a relative increase in poverty, look likely to rage on in the pages of learned journals. Yet these attempts to identify what has changed to turn the underclass into such an important issue all seem to miss the central point.

Whatever the microeconomic trends may or may not be, the fact is that the microeconomic status of the impoverished Black communities of the inner cities has not altered enough to justify all of the renewed debate about an emergent Black underclass. The fact that analysts can detect the incomes of urban Black communities shifting a few percentage points up or down the scale may have consequences for those who are directly affected, but it does not qualitatively transform the position of inner-city Blacks in relation to the rest of American society. The poor are still the poor; and the Black poor are still generally the poorest of the poor.

The key thing that has changed in the last few years is not the reality of Black poverty. It is the dominant *response* to that poverty from politicians and other experts which has been transformed. It is not the way in which the Black inner-city communities live but the way in which their lives are viewed and treated by those in authority that has truly undergone a fundamental change.

The changing response to urban poverty, like the other developments in the discussion of race-related issues, reflects the renewed ascendancy of racial thinking in the U.S political system today. It is this shift in the political mood, rather than any changing patterns of life in the inner city, that explains why the concept of the underclass has come to such prominence of late.

The notion of a Black underclass is a politically loaded label, which conservatives have developed in order to shift the responsibility for poverty and degradation onto the backs of the Black inner-city communities themselves. The concept of the underclass represents a repackaging of traditional right-wing prejudices about the poor and Blacks in the language of modern sociology. It is an artificial construction of the new racial thinkers. And it is one, moreover, that has been adopted by the most prominent spokesmen of the liberal intelligentsia.

Here we come to what has changed most of all—the political and intellectual climate in which the debate about the causes of Black poverty takes place. The extent to which the term "underclass" is now used by commentators of all political persuasions reflects the long-term success of conservatism in setting the contemporary agenda in America. It is illustrative of the emergence of a post-liberal consensus on matters of race among social policymakers.

Conservative comments on the Black underclass generally focus on the problem of the "culture of poverty." Stripped of the jargon, the basic argument of the culture-of-poverty thesis is that the Black "underclass" is impoverished and deprived, not because of the way in which society is organized, but primarily because of its own bad behavior. Thus, according to conservative wisdom, the position of Blacks in inner cities is defined and reinforced by the "pathologies" of the underclass, by its "dysfunctional attitudes," and by its departure from the "norms and mores of the American way of life."

The only way in which conservatives try to implicate the social system in the problem is to say that since the dark radical days of the sixties, governments have tried to do *too much* to nanny impoverished Blacks. The consequence of over-generous welfare pay-outs has apparently been to reinforce the culture of poverty with its rejection of the work ethic and its indulgence of unmarried mothers living on government checks.

We shall need to examine further the implications of the conservative assault on the culture of poverty, and the dangers of the way in which liberal opinion has adapted to this discussion. But first, let us touch briefly upon some of the arguments that are routinely used to suggest that the behavior and "pathology" of the Black underclass is to blame for many of the serious problems facing the inner-city communities. It may then become easier to understand the extent to which the "underclass" is an artificial product of modern political thought.

DEVIANT BEHAVIOR

Those leading the ideological war against the "underclass" are always at pains to point out that they have no argument with people such as the elderly or the infirm or the temporarily unemployed, who may be poor through no fault of their own. Their target is that subsection of the U.S. poor who are marked out as a race apart, not by their poverty alone, but by their elective "underclass behavior." This behavior is considered unacceptable because, as a reflection of the culture of poverty, it departs from what the conservatives claim are the accepted mores of American life.

One of the most prominent exponents of the culture-of-poverty thesis is Charles Murray of the American Enterprise Institute. In one of several scathing pieces he wrote in response to the 1992 Los Angeles riots, Murray sought to spell out what those mores were, in order to indicate where the welfare-subsidized Black underclass of the American inner city had fallen short of the standard:

"It turns out that communities survive by socializing their young to certain norms of behavior. They achieve that socialization with the help of realities to which parents can point—you have to work, or you won't eat; if you don't have a husband, you won't be able to take care of your children; if you commit crimes, you will go to jail...Outside the inner city, we are busily reconstructing the damage done to the social fabric during the reform period of the sixties, with considerable success. Inside the inner city, that fabric has become so tattered that it is difficult to see any external means of restoration."[5]

The same emphasis on the fact that people in general live by the laws and rules of society, and the suggestion that the underclass has created its own problems by failing to do so, is evident in many other conservative commentaries. Thus Isabel V. Sawhill argues that "In America today certain mores are widely held." She says that America expects children to study hard, expects young people to refrain from having children until they can support them, expects adults to work at a steady job, and expects everyone to obey the laws:

"These are social obligations. Those who fulfill them are unlikely to be chronically poor. If they are poor despite having abided by the rules, society is much more likely to come to their rescue. This is and (with the possible exception of the 1960s) always has been the nature of the social contract. The problem is too many people who are not fulfilling their end of the bargain: these people constitute the Underclass."[6]

So the idea, broadly, is that decent Americans live by the rules and fulfill their social obligations, while a deviant minority refuses to do so and indulges instead in "underclass behavior." That is essentially why some people do okay, while others are chronically poor. It looks like a straightforward enough distinction on paper. But look up from the page at the realities of life in America today, and things appear a little less clear-cut.

The underclass is said to create its own problems by departing from the standards that are set in the national "norms of behavior." Therefore, anybody who breaks these rules surely ought to be included in the anti-social minority of the underclass. But it doesn't seem to work out that way.

Take for example some of the features of "underclass behavior" that are most commonly identified by conservatives: laziness, love of the latest fads and fashions, drug addition and alcohol abuse, an easy attitude to sexual relationships, and a lack of commitment to marital stability. To conservatives, that might be a catalogue of the sort of unique underclass "pathologies" that are to be found in places like South Central Los Angeles. To me it sounds like a description of how the very rich live and die up in places like Beverly Hills. Yet, strangely, nobody has seen fit to launch a major sociological debate about "the problem of the OVERclass" in America today. These things only seem to be considered a threat to the fabric of society when they are linked with the poor.

And what of the "norms of behavior" listed by the conservative commentators quoted above? Norms like "You have to do a decent day's work or you won't eat." Try telling that to William Kennedy Smith and his preppie friends. Or suggest it to the Wall Street financial operators, whose way of life was summed up by Gordon Gecko in Oliver Stone's movie "Wall Street": "I create nothing. I own things." And what about another "norm," like "If you break the law you will go to jail." It is not applied quite so equally and enforceably to gun-runners connected with the White House, or to policemen who beat up Black motorists, or to many of those who make their millions through fraud, tax evasion, and other modern business methods.

The conservatives want to prove that those whom they have branded as the "Black underclass" deviate from "norms" and "mores" that are upheld by everybody else in decent American society. In order for this to be proven, however, the poor have to be judged by very different "norms" or standards than those which their accusers would apply to others at the top end of the social scale. Behind all of the present-day academic discourse on the underclass, it appears, then, as if the message from the powerful to the powerless is much the same as it was a century ago: "Do as we say, not as we do." The notion of "underclass behavior" has become a political device with which to blame impoverished Blacks for the inequalities in American society.

In order to sustain the culture-of-poverty thesis, the lives of the "underclass" also have to be effectively removed from any proper socioeconomic context. How else can conservatives seriously argue, at a time of permanent mass unemployment, that these people are unemployed, not because there are few jobs, but because they lack the work ethic of Middle America?

Through all the studies and investigations of recent years, nobody has ever been able to demonstrate that people on welfare in America's inner cities have a "pathological" unwillingness to work for a decent wage. Every survey or interview conducted among ghetto youth reflects their desire for "good jobs" to provide an escape from the criminal sub-economy. Yet conservatives continually berate the young men of the "Black underclass" for failing to appear gratefully enthusiastic about the dim prospect of obtaining what is euphemistically called "entry-level employment."

It is hardly surprising that young Blacks do not see a $4-an-hour job in a store or in a workfare-style "training" scheme as the key to a better future—especially when they know that, for them, the "entry-level" and "exit-level" of such a career are likely to be the same level—the bottom. This veiwpoint is simply a recognition of material realities for those at the wrong end of the economic pile. It is a practical example of the unequal relationship to the process of wealth production and distribution that is the foundation of racial discrimination in contemporary America. Yet for the conservatives, it is a sign of "dysfunctional behavior." Once more, in order to prove their culture-of-poverty thesis, these conservatives have to apply seriously distorted double standards.

For instance, in the recessionary economic climate of recent years, many American businessmen are not very keen to invest in industry, to put their capital to work, because they do not think they will get a worthwhile return for their trouble. They would rather allow their money to "lounge about" in banks, bonds, or stocks. Yet there has been no outcry about the dangers of a "culture of profitability," or the problems caused by "pathological underinvestment." Instead, the unadventurous attitude of these venture capitalists is seen as common sense, as a reasonable response to the economic realities of their situation. When it comes to examining Black youth's unenthusiastic response to the idea of performing soul-destroying drudgery in return for peanuts, however, the tone changes completely, and the sanctimonious talk is all about the culture of poverty and the pathology of the idle underclass.

UNHAPPY FAMILIES

The crisis of the Black family is a commonplace subject of conservative attacks upon the "underclass." The high numbers of families headed by a single mother within inner-city communities is held up as a particularly deep problem. According to the conservative point of view, this is another aspect of the culture of poverty. The "dysfunctional family" of the ghetto, they claim, has been produced by the slack sexual morality and lack of respect for the marital state that typify "underclass behavior." And that behavior, complain the conservative commentators, has been endorsed and sponsored by the extension of welfare payments to unmarried mothers, which make it unnecessary and perhaps even disadvantageous for them to get married.

This problem of the dysfunctional family is also supposed to have important spin-off effects on the behavior of Black "underclass" males. Freed from the responsibilities of family life, the adult male is supposed to become a shifty, work-shy drifter, living in a netherworld of drink, drugs, and sex. Without the strong hand of a diligent father to keep him on the straight and narrow, the young ghetto male is expected to follow the same path to a life of crime, drugs, and casual sex.

This viewpoint has been expounded in slightly different forms for some 30 years. Back in 1965, Daniel P. Moynihan observed that fatherless children were a particular problem of the "Negro family": "White children without fathers at least perceive all about them the pattern of men working. Negro children without fathers flounder—and fail."[7] Thirty years on, that view has been accepted as a matter of common sense, with one crucial difference. Where Moynihan then saw the crisis of the "Negro family" as a consequence of racial discrimination and a problem requiring social action and support, the view from the top downwards today is that Black family breakdown is a consequence of "underclass" behavior, which can only be tackled through moral lectures about family values and cuts in welfare payments to single parents.

What is really behind the debate about family breakdown in America? It is certainly true that breakdown and conflict within the family is a common and often tragic feature of life for sections of American society today. Take the unhappy case of the "R" family as an example.

Neither Mr. R nor Mrs. R had been raised in a stable two-parent family. Mrs. R's own father had walked out on her mother. Mr. R's father was an alcoholic. Mr. R himself already had one marital breakdown behind him. The unhappiness of their own family life has been at least partly revealed by their daughter. It is a familiar tale of violence and drugs, of a domineering mother and a father living in a fantasy world, of lies and endless rows about money.

"As uncomfortable as it is to talk about, and write about, abuse is part of this story. I first remember my mother hitting me when I was eight. It escalated as I got older and became a weekly, sometimes daily event...Later, my father comes in...'Why is she mean to me?' 'She never is.' 'Well, why does she hit me?' 'Patti, that never happened.'

"Over the years, the name of the drug would change, but the behavior wouldn't...I have to look now at my history and particularly my long battle with my mother in the context of her pills...I now feel her unpredictable moods, her ability to alter facts at will, may be related to the pills she took over the years...I later became a drug addict. Like my mother, I got pills from doctors...One of my prayers, when I was around ten, was that my parents would get divorced and I'd get to live with my father."[8]

And so it goes on. It sounds like a tale of the breakdown of traditional family values, of the kind which the American Right has been keen to highlight over the past decade. The Republican Party has not, however, used this particular example in its publicity. Which is probably not too surprising, given that the family in question was supposed to be America's First Family; Mr. and Mrs. R. Reagan and their children.

The conservatives claim that the poverty and deprivation suffered by the "Black underclass" is at least caused by the prevalence of the "dysfunctional family" in the ghetto. That notion has to rest upon the assumption that a normal or "functional" pattern of stable family life is to be found among other, better-off sections of American society. However, as the case of the Reagans indicates, the happy nuclear family is not quite as all-American as the critics of the "underclass" would like to imply that it is.

For just about everybody, family life is a tense and sometimes deeply unhappy affair. People living closely together in unequal relationships, in an atmosphere fraught with all of the explosive ingredients of emotion, sex, money, and personal power, always have the potential to lash out at each other and tear the fragile family structure apart. For the women at the center of it all, who normally have to carry the bulk of the responsibility for holding things together, family life can be an intolerable burden.

How different people handle the strains of the family relationship is not just a question of their personal attitudes; it is largely a matter of their personal circumstances. To sustain at least an appearance of stable or "functional" family life, a certain level of material stability is required.

It was relatively easy for the millionaire Reagans to keep up appearances as the happy American family, with their luxurious home to hide in and their PR agents to promote the right image of family bliss. This option is not generally open to members of the Black or Latino communities living in places like South Central Los Angeles or the South Bronx.

For those living on or below the poverty line in the grim tenements and rented rooms of the inner city, there is no place to hide from the pressures of family life, and no money with which to paper over the cracks. The results are pretty inevitable.

The tensions that exist in every family will always have a disproportionate impact on family structure among those who have least to fall back on, whether they are Blacks in Los Angeles, California or poor Whites in Liverpool, England. What's different in America today is that the failure of impoverished Blacks to match up to the Right's image of family life is being used to help explain why these Blacks are poor in the first place. Instead of poverty and degradation being seen as strong contributory factors in the problems of these families, these conditions are described as consequences of the departure from "normal" family values in the ghetto.

Conservatives try to turn reality on its head, by claiming that it is actually the *surplus* of easy money in the inner city that has led to the breakdown of traditional family life. The idea that liberal welfare payments to unmarried mothers have helped to bring this situation about is nothing more than right-wing prejudice—and one that is so strongly held that it appears it cannot be shaken even when all the evidence points in another direction. Here is Isabel Sawhill again, putting mere facts in their place:

"To be sure, real welfare benefits have fallen by 37 percent since 1970, at a time when the Underclass has grown, and researchers have found little correlation between state benefit levels and the proportion of families headed by women. But it is hard to imagine that the availability of this reasonably steady, albeit small income has had no impact on life in inner-city communities."[9]

That can only be "hard to imagine" for somebody who has never had the pleasure of trying to raise a family on welfare checks that are falling in value, and is prepared to ignore all the evidence in pursuit of his argument.

The notion that there is a newly "dysfunctional" Black family that deviates from the national norm also ignores the changes which both the image and the reality of family life has undergone all across the United States in recent years.

For example, social changes have brought a growth in the number of single-parent families, not only among the poor of the inner cities, but in every racial and socio-economic segment of American society. The White middle-class mother who is either divorced or has never married is now a fairly common phenomenon. Yet these women do not attract the sort of criticism reserved for the impoverished single mothers who are designated part of the "underclass." Nobody seriously suggests that the economic status of the women in the first group has been caused by their lack of a husband.

It was very noticeable that when Vice President Dan Quayle made his notorious speeches about "family values" after the 1992 Los Angeles riots, his criticism of the sitcom character Murphy Brown, a prestigious television anchorwoman who decides to have a baby out of wedlock, got him into the worst trouble. Quayle's attack on the loose morals of unmarried ghetto mothers was considerably less controversial. The point here is not to criticize unmarried mothers who have a decent income; if only it were so for all women who are raising children alone. The double standards that inform the debate about single-parent families, however, offer another important clue to the way in which a hidden class and racial agenda is being pursued in relation to criticisms of the "underclass."

The conservative critique of the "dysfunctional underclass family" also ignores the extent to which the post war image of the all-American family has been widely tarnished by the experience of the past 20 years. The shiny, smiling pictures of the 1950s family—White skin, White teeth, huge White icebox—reflected a time of economic expansion, when more families than ever before could afford to be happy—or at least to acquire the consumerist symbols of contentment.

Today all that has changed for most Americans. Just about the only thing that the average American family of the early nineties has in common with that of the fifties is their income, since in real terms incomes have now fallen back to their lowest levels in more than 30 years. It is widely accepted today that the average young couple is unlikely to ever be as well off as their parents were and that just about their only chance of owning a nice home is to inherit the one in which they were born.

As these harsher circumstances shape people's lives, that perfect family picture loses its shine. The contemporary media images of family life which strike a chord among many Americans are no longer provided by *I Love Lucy* or *Father Knows Best* but by Homer, Bart, and the rest of the Simpsons. In seeking to blame the position of poor Blacks on the so-called underclass behavior of their dysfunctional families, conservatives are comparing them unfavorably with a model family that no longer exists—if indeed it ever really did.

WHY DO BLACKS LAG BEHIND KOREANS?

There is another elitist argument about the existence of a Black underclass, an argument that relates most directly to the question of race. The argument is that the behavior and "culture" of inner-city Blacks must help to account for their lowly status, because they are lagging behind the achievements of other non-White communities that have been in America for a far shorter period of time.

The conservative argument has gathered renewed force since the Los Angeles riots, when the media highlighted conflicts between Korean storekeepers and their Black and Latino customers in South Central Los Angeles. The images of Uzi-carrying Korean businessmen protecting their premises from a mob of wicked looters were paraded before the American public as further evidence that the criminally minded Black "underclass" is stuck at the bottom of the ladder by its own unwillingness to climb in the way that the Koreans have done.

In an article on the LA unrest entitled "How the Rioters Won," Midge Decter railed against the envious and idle Black "underclass," and against the White liberals who refused to confront underclass "hatred" of the Koreans: "It is the hatred felt for the enterprising immigrants in their midst by individuals living month to month on government checks, unable to do for themselves or by themselves."[10]

Not for the first time, Charles Murray took this point further than other commentators in the post-Los Angeles debate. He combined his regular attack upon the "advantages" given to Blacks since the sixties with a scathing attack upon the failure of American Blacks to match the achievements of others. The result was a composite argument of the new racial thinking about the Black underclass: "It is not racism—not racism in the old sense at any rate—to conclude that Blacks have in truth been given a number of advantages for more than 20 years. It is not the old style of racism to conclude that the present problems of the Black community owe more to Black behavior than to White oppression. And it is ABOVE ALL not racism to look at the unaided achievements of poor Asian immigrants—and the unaided achievements of poor Caribbean immigrants, poor Nigerian immigrants, poor Ethiopian immigrants—and ask: 'If they can do it, why can't American Blacks?' It is a legitimate question, requiring more than glib answers about the legacy of slavery."[11]

Murray is right; his arguments against the "underclass" are not crude "racism in the old sense." They underpin the new, apparently more sophisticated politics of race. In this context, Murray's last little barb against "glib answers about the legacy of slavery" was well aimed. There has for too long been a tendency for critics of racism in America to try to ascribe the difficulties faced by Black people today to the treatment their forefathers endured in the eighteenth and nineteenth centuries. But blaming history is an unrealistic response, and one which can look like an attempt to sidestep the questions posed by people like Murray in the present. So is there another way to meet Murray's challenge about the failure of the "Black underclass" to keep pace with other, newer minority groups in America?

A preliminary point worth noting is that the economic success of a community like the Koreans is relative rather than absolute; it is only impressive when put next to the position of the Black and Latino poor. The Koreans, too, have suffered a degree of discrimination. They have certainly not been allowed access to full membership in the WASP-run American business class. If they had, they would not have been left running corner liquor stores and gas stations in the most derelict corners of Los Angeles. And running them, moreover, in the most perilous of financial positions. According to the president of LA's biggest Korean bank, "The average Korean business owner in Los Angeles is somewhere between $200,000 and $500,000 in debt. Like most minority business owners, they also tend to have no insurance or to be underinsured."[12] The "business success" which American society allowed those Koreans was thus of the type that could be wiped out with one molotov cocktail.

However, it remains true that the Koreans ran those stores and the local Blacks didn't. But that situation should not be read as evidence to support the culture-of-poverty thesis or the case against the "underclass." Instead, what the Korean experience reveals is the impact of immigration on American society. And what the debate about Korean-Black conflicts reveals is the way in which the new politics of race can be used to legitimize modern inequalities and set communities against one another.

Immigrant groups are always among the most dynamic and thrusting sections of society. It is a case of the newcomers striving to get a foothold, to be accepted. Nowhere is this more obvious than in the United States, the most immigrant-based country of them all. In the past, the millions of immigrants drawn in by the promise of America's tremendous economic expansion became the thrusting foot soldiers of the "frontier spirit." Things are very different in today's age of economic stagnation. Yet it is still the case that new immigrant groups, from Korea and elsewhere, will generally be the most active in trying to get one rung up from the bottom of the ladder.

This is part of the explanation as to why the new groups of Black immigrants that Murray mentions—the Nigerians, the Ethiopians, and Caribbean Islanders—can also do better than indigenous American Blacks for a generation or two. If it were truly a question of "culture" making most American Blacks unfit for success, then this culture would surely also condemn these groups immediately to the ghetto. After all, Africans from Ethiopia and Nigeria certainly do not comply with the "mores" of American society that the conservatives are always talking about. And many members of a group like Caribbean Islanders have far more in common with the so-called underclass culture of inner-city Blacks than they do either with mainstream American life or with the ways of the Koreans. Yet their status as newcomers allows them the chances to get at least one step ahead of American Blacks.

The flipside of the immigrant experience is that of the older, indigenous groups at the wrong end of American society. Here, the reality is that the poor stay poor, whether they are Black or White. For those who have been trapped at the bottom of the economic pile propping up the rest, there is no escape. There is no way for the average Black youth from South Central Los Angeles to become something as modest as a local store-keeper; indeed, there is no reason why he should even think it is worth trying to achieve such a thing.

This has nothing to do with some sort of innate shortcomings among Black Americans. After all, much the same is true of that longstanding group of White urban poor, the Irish Americans. They too were left close to the bottom for generations, while other, newer immigrants—even including new waves of immigration from Ireland—have moved a notch above them. By focusing on the failures of the Black community, however, the authorities have managed to contain the Irish

Americans by convincing many of them that at least they are better than the "niggers."

The racial thinking of people like Murray allows the authorities to legitimize the inequalities in American society and to divide the disadvantaged against each other. The culture-of-poverty thesis suggests that American Blacks are at the bottom only because of their own behavioral problems. The implication is that those groups, other than the Black "underclass," who do obey the rules and live by the "mores and norms" of American society can get ahead.

And even if "getting ahead" only means being a storekeeper up to your neck in debt, or holding down a white-collar clerical job, it is still possible to consider yourself a success in comparison to American Blacks. Through their theory of the culture of poverty and their hypocritical praise for the achievements of new immigrants, the conservative elites are seeking to keep alive a glimmer of the American dream in conditions of economic decline. For many in modern America, the limit of economic ambition has become, not to reach the heights of middle-class prosperity, but at least to rise a step or two above the Black underclass.

Of course, the tensions between Blacks and Koreans or other immigrant groups were not invented by Charles Murray or by the media. There is no way on Earth that Korean shopkeepers can be considered the major cause of problems facing Black people in the ghetto. But they are at the cutting edge of the friction between the Black community and the system. For many frustrated Black youths, the Koreans appear to be the most visible local symbol of the wealthy and exploitative city outside the ghetto. They live in another, better neighborhood, drive to work in a new Jeep, refuse you credit, charge you too much, and treat you like a thief. Lashing out at them is a misdirected attempt to hit back at what keeps you down.

Reactionary politicians, media commentators, and other conservatives have a vested interest in overemphasizing the importance of conflicts between Blacks and Koreans, or more recently between Blacks and immigrants from Mexico and Central America. These tensions give them the opportunity to turn the spotlight away from the central issue of racial discrimination, to the side issue of inter-communal conflict. It provides the elites with the chance to focus on the symptoms rather than the causes of the inner-city's problems, and to pursue the politics of divide-and-conquer.

Better still, by playing up the hatred that Black youth are said to feel for Koreans, the Right is able to accuse the Blacks themselves of perpetrating racism! Racial prejudice is thereby transformed from something used against minorities by the powerful elites at the top of society to something that the poor Blacks at the bottom display against others. Such is the scale of the distortions and falsehoods that are sustained by the whole debate about the conservatives' favorite invention of our times—the Black urban "underclass."

Having tried to indicate some of the ways in which the notion of a "Black underclass" has been constructed, let us return to examine again the purpose that it plays for the conservative elites. In doing so, we may be able to answer the big question: why are they able to get away with it?

THE IMMORALITY OF INDIVIDUALS

A central attraction of the "underclass" concept from the conservative point of view is that it separates poverty from its social causes. Once poverty has been separated from its social causes, you quickly arrive at the second consequence of the "underclass" debate: the transformation of a social problem into a moral one. The U.S. government and business elites are exonerated of all blame for the plight of those at the bottom. Instead, immoral individuals who behave badly must bear the responsibility.

The consequence of the "underclass" debate and the culture-of-poverty thesis is that nothing much can be done to help the Black poor. Thus the new wisdom has it that there is no point throwing money at the problem. Indeed, say the conservatives, there's been too much of that already. Which is why Charles Murray and his co-thinkers call for welfare to be cut back or ended altogether. Instead of money, it seems, what the Black communities of the inner city need is a proper moral code. Respect for authority, hard work, thrift and self-denial—these are the values that the Right claims that the "underclass" needs if it is to be saved from itself.

Ever since the emergence of industrial capitalism, there have been debates about the causes of poverty. The conservative defenders of the status quo have consistently rejected the idea that such problems were due to the way society has been organized. Instead, they have argued, the problem is the failing of the individual. For much of the modern age, these arguments have been publicly upheld only by a minority. Now, however, they appear to be gathering strength once more, and the "Who's to blame?" debate is back with a vengeance.

The sort of arguments we hear about the Black underclass today take on a very contemporary, sophisticated shape. Yet the underlying ideas are in many ways a throwback to the reactionary themes of racial politics in the nineteenth century. Over the past 40 years or so, however, American society has generally considered these arguments unsuitable for public airing.

After the riots of the 1960s, for example, conservative attempts to blame poverty on the behavior of Black inner-city communities held very little weight. Key contributions to the debate about social policy, such as the report of the Werner Commission, acknowledged the connection between social factors and poverty as a simple matter of common sense. The view that the poor were to blame for their predicament was very much a minority outlook on the fringes of political and intellectual life in the sixties.

Edward Banfield's classic conservative statement *The Un-heavenly : The Nature and Future of our Urban Crisis,* published in 1968, foreshadowed many of the themes of today's discussion. Banfield argued in up-front fashion that the inner cities were no good because the people who lived there were no good. The poor lacked the middle-class ethos of hard work, family values, personal hygiene, saving money, etc., and so nothing could be done to save them. At the time, these ideas were fairly isolated and uninfluential in public debate. A quarter of a century later, however, when neo-conservative organizations such as the American Enterprise Institute present similar ideas about the "Black underclass" causing its own problems, these ideas are given a place at the very center of American political discourse. Indeed, when the AEI published Michael Novak's *A Community of Self-Reliance* in 1987, the institute felt able to give it the rather grandiose subtitle "The New Consensus on Family and Wel-fare."

The discussion of the "underclass problem" in the 1990s reflects the change in the intellectual and political climate in America. The main point to come out of all of the arguments and opinion exchanges is that unrest such as the riots in Los Angeles has far more to do with morality than with poverty. The real evil is therefore the act of riot, not the degradation of human life in the ghetto.

Of course, many conservative commentators have had to acknowledge the fact that people do endure dire conditions in the inner cities. But the essential message from these self-appointed spokesmen for public opinion is that the American people can live with a little poverty and deprivation (although not too closely, please). But what we cannot tolerate is the malevolence of the underclass. While paying brief lip service to the structural problems of the inner city, the conservatives must play down the social factors that create poverty about and emphasize instead that the cause of the problem is the BREAKDOWN OF THE MORAL CODE.

The reorientation of the post-riot discussion in this fashion helps to divert attention away from a critique of American society. The fact that the conservative opinionmakers have been able to achieve this so successfully, despite the glaring weaknesses in many of their own arguments, demonstrates the extent to which traditional liberal ideas have now been marginalized. After the riots of the sixties, the liberal emphasis on society having to take some of the blame for what happened to the Black communities was the dominant view. Even ten years ago, these types of arguments remained pretty influential. Today, however, they are decidedly unfashionable.

THE END OF LIBERALISM

American liberalism has not lost out because of the all-powerful logic of the conservative case. As we have already indicated, much conservative "analysis" is at root little more than old-fashioned prejudice dressed up with modern jargon. Instead, the spokesmen of liberalism themselves have suffered something of an inner moral collapse. They have proved incapable of standing up to the conservative counter-attack and have conceded ground hand-over-fist to the arguments of their opponents. The most striking thing about liberal criticisms of the culture-of-poverty thesis today, for example, is the extent to which they share many of the assumptions about the "underclass" that underpin the conservative case.

One of the most prominent liberal critics of the culture-of-poverty thesis in recent years has been William Julius Wilson, most notably in his *The Truly Disadvantaged.*[13] Wilson's analysis of the crisis in the innner cities puts most emphasis on the uneven impact that changes in the American and global economy have upon these areas. He demonstrates that the movement of manufacturing jobs out of the cities has left behind pockets of abject poverty and created the urban "underclass."

Wilson's emphasis upon how external socioeconomic factors have helped to wreck the inner cities may seem to be a direct challenge to the conservative interpretation of events. But if we look at his arguments a little closer, a different picture emerges. Wilson's point is that these socioeconomic trends are to blame not only for deepening poverty but for the emergence of behavioral and attitudinal "pathologies" among the "underclass." He says that the circumstances in which the poor live lead them to act in "deviant" ways.

In other words, Wilson is primarily interested in addressing the same issue as the conservatives: the "underclass behavior" of inner-city residents. In substance, if not in form, many of his arguments are thus compatible with the broad drift of the culture-of-poverty thesis. He identifies a different cause of the problem, and suggests a different solution. But he is essentially operating from the same premise and seeking to address the same problem—the way that the "underclass" behaves, rather than the way in which the American system works.

In this, Wilson's arguments are fairly representative of the way that liberal critics have conceded the central points of the conservative case. They disagree with the Right's moral crusade against the "underclass" only inasmuch as they believe that social deprivation creates the conditions where human wrongdoing can thrive. In their response to the conservatives, the spokespersons of mainstream American liberalism are in fact seeking different solutions to the same problem—the supposed problem of moral laxity among the Black "underclass"—instead of to the material shortcomings of American society.

The consequence of this coalescence is that, in the aftermath of what were arguably the worst modern American riots, there has really been no serious consideration of urban impoverishment. Instead, we have witnessed a post-liberal consensus start to emerge through a wide-ranging discussion around the conservatives' moral agenda: family values, parental discipline, delinquent children, and so on.

The terms of this debate had already been prefigured by the collapse of the old liberal camp. Senator Daniel Patrick Moynihan was the leading light in the liberal Democratic administrations of the sixties, and one of the intellectual forces behind the War on Poverty. Over the past few years, however, Moynihan has radically altered his assessment about the balance to be struck today between individual and social causes of deprivation. He has also issued some remarkably defensive and apologetic revisions of the attitudes he expressed in the sixties.

Moynihan has noted, for example, how in 1964 he wrote a speech with which President Johnson was to introduce a report which found that one-third of American youth would fail to qualify for military service. LBJ had told the press corps that "poverty is the principal reason why these young men fail to meet those physical and mental standards." Moynihan is now amazed and embarrassed that he could ever have penned such an explanation of the poor's failure:

"Why did I write that this was the result of poverty? Why did I not write that poverty was the result of THIS? Ignorance, as Dr. Johnson observed...I was surely no Marxist...Yet I thought, as a good Madisonian, that the 'various and unequal distribution of property' accounted for many social phenomena. What I had not adequately grasped was the degree to which these unequal distributions of property were in turn dependent upon a still more powerful agent—the behavior of individuals and communities."[14]

Although Moynihan is shocked that he could have held such views in the past, the fact is that for the past 40 years it would have been shocking for him to think anything else. The link between society and inequality was obvious to all but the most prejudice-blinded bigot. Today, however, the conservatives are redefining common sense and rewriting the past. And it is the surrender of old leading liberals like Moynihan that has made their vacuous arguments appear so powerful, and so made their task relatively straightforward.

This points us towards an important observation. The success of the new crusade against the Black "underclass" does not rest upon its own dynamism and intellectual power; it really has nothing new to say. Instead, it has been built upon the discrediting and the internal collapse of the old alternatives, and the convergence of liberalism with conservatism in the elitist consensus of today.

Under the Democratic administration of Bill Clinton, for example, the liberal sections of the political and intellectual elites have joined the moral crusade to scapegoat the "underclass" for social problems. Clinton himself has emphasized the importance of "individual responsibility" among the poor—which translates into a shifting of responsibility away from government and a case for more welfare cuts.

The case for family values has also been taken up by erstwhile liberal voices from the communitarian and centrist lobbies. "Dan Quayle was right," announced *Atlantic Monthly* magazine in April 1993. Through bodies like the Institute for American Values, liberal academics have replaced clerics as the most powerful lobbyists for a return to traditional two-parent family values in the ghetto. Clinton himself, a year after being elected to turn back the tide of Republican policymakers, was praising Dan Quayle's infamous anti-single-mothers speech. And would his administration prefer children to be raised in nuclear families? "You bet we would."[15]

Perhaps most telling of all was the conversion of Donna Shalala, Clinton's Secretary of Health and Human Services and the administration's token progressive feminist. "I don't like to put this in moral terms," she said in 1994, and then went on to do so: "but I do believe that having babies out of wedlock is just wrong."[16] The elitist notion that single mothers on welfare are immoral, and that they are at least partly responsible for social problems from poverty to crime, and need to be dealt with by authoritarian measures such as orphanages, workfare, or even jail now stretches across the political and intellectual spectrum.

Whatever their subjective intentions may be, those who help to convert social problems into moral ones will always end up pointing the finger at the individual. Society does not have to bear any responsibility for any breakdown of moral code. The idea of immorality is always about individuals and their failures. Once they have made that key concession, the liberals converge with the conservatives in an elitist bloc to blame the Black poor for the problems created by the American social system.

Despite all of the sociological jargon, the discussion of the "Black underclass" represents, then, the moral condemnation of the urban poor by the powerful U.S. elites. Through the application of distorted standards, members of the "underclass" have been cast as wicked individuals in an otherwise acceptable American society. This is a particularly nice image with which to flatter the conservative imagination, since these individuals are not just evil, they are also inferior to respectable citizens. You can almost hear the sneer in Midge Decter's voice as he looks down his nose at the inferior Black youth of the inner city: "How is it possible for anyone to look at these boys of the underclass—to look at them, literally, with one's own eyes, and actually SEE them—and imagine that they either want or could hold on to jobs?"[17]

That such crude, simplistic, and racially based accounts of human behavior can now be aired in public demonstrates how the elitist ideas of the nineteenth century are making something of a comeback. The new conservatives feel obliged to talk in code, emphasizing not racial differences as such but "cultural" differences that set the Black "underclass" apart from and keep it below the rest of society. But coded or not, the basic message is the same, and it serves to bolster the authority of those atop American society at the expense of those at the bottom.

6. THE BLACK RESPONSE

How has the elite's manipulation of the race issue impacted upon the prevalent attitudes and outlooks within the Black community itself?

In practical terms, the combination of institutionalized discrimination with the politicization of the racial divide has reinforced a contemporary system of segregation. The inner cities of America have largely become containment zones for Black and other minority communities. Impoverished Blacks are now increasingly marginalized within American society. Through a combined strategy of welfare spending cuts and militarized policing, the inner cities where these people live have been turned into "third worlds within." As a former member of the Los Angeles Crips gang puts it, "I wish someone would tell me the difference between Guatemala and South Central."[1] Like Guatemala, the ghettos seem a million miles from the suburbs of Middle America.

In political terms, the emergence of a post-liberal consensus on issues relating to race and social policy has transformed the climate in which Black communities relate to American society. In this harsh climate, Black communities can readily be blamed for creating their own problems, while little attention is paid to the social causes of poverty and unemployment. The key political device for shifting blame onto the shoulders of poor Blacks is the doctrine of individual responsibility. Moreover, the post-liberal consensus has turned reality entirely on its head. Black people are not only blamed for causing the problems of the inner city but are even held responsible for the wider problems of American society, through panics about crime, drugs, and family breakdown.

In effect, the U.S. elites have told the Black poor to go and stand in a corner and behave themselves, or face more serious punishment.

The combined effect of these two developments has had a serious impact upon Black communities. The majority of Black people feel even more isolated from the rest of U.S. society today than they did previously. Their bitter sense of alienation has been considerably heightened. At the same time, the convergence of American liberalism with the conservative agenda has thrown traditional anti-racism onto the defensive.

The consequences of all this for Black attitudes are serious. An increasingly common response to the experience of relative isolation is now for Black leaders to become defensive and turn their attention inward. More and more of the problems identified and the solutions proposed by Black leaders today tend to focus, not upon the nature of U.S. society, but rather upon the internal affairs of the Black community itself.

In other words, as America's ruling elites have turned their backs on Blacks and their concerns, so more Black people have turned away from the wider American society in their search for a solution to their own problems. And as more American leaders have propagated the doctrine of individual responsibility, so many Black spokespersons have accepted that Black communities have to stop complaining about inequality and put their own house in order. The elitist inversion of the reality of racial issues in America today has even come to exert a leading influence over discussion within the Black community itself.

This fashionable inward-looking Black perspective can now be found in both conservative and radical forms. But it is always problematic—in particular, because turning our attention inward in such an insular way tends to legitimize the ghettoization of Black people and their problems. It makes it easier for the political elites to set the agenda on race in relation to crime and the "underclass" debate, and to keep the real issues of racial discrimination and inequality out of the center of public debate in America. In effect, it means that when the U.S. elites tell Black people to stand in the corner, Black leaders respond by saying that's where they want to be anyway.

Let's consider the problems this might cause in relation to some Black perspectives that have been proposed and adopted in recent debates.

THE "BLACKLASH"

Over the pat few years, we have witnessed the emergence of a powerful new and conservative current in Black responses to the problems of inner-city areas. It is a reaction against liberal interpretations of urban poverty and other problems, and it has become known among some commentators as the "Blacklash." In effect, it represents the conservative argument about the Black poor being responsible for their own problems, only posed in language that is more acceptable and accessible to a Black audience.

The basic thesis of the "Blacklash" school of argument is that Black communities in American cities should stop trying to blame outside forces for the desperate problems that they face in the nineties. It is no good, say the Black-lashers, continually droning on about racial discrimination, police harassment, economic apartheid and similar themes. Instead, Blacks need to face up to the fact that many of their problems have been generated from within their own communities. And having faced up to that fact, they need to do something about changing this sad state of affairs.

The Blacklash has been shaped by the elites' insistence that many of the most serious problems confronting Black America today have little to do with the way in which the broader social-economic-political system functions in this country. The problems that did once exist at that level have supposedly been largely resolved through legislation and formal desegregation. Now what needs to be addressed most urgently are the moral shortcomings of the individual members of Black inner-city communities. The children of the ghetto need to be taught to behave like decent American citizens.

The Black political scientist Glen Loury has summed up one Blacklash argument with a call for Black people in the inner cities to take individual responsibility for resolving their difficulties. "The problem of the Black underclass," says Loury, "is a problem that will only be solved one by one and from the inside out."[2] Other Black spokespersons and legislators have focused on the problem of crime among Black youth as the key issue which needs to be addressed. Thus Black political representatives from areas such as South Central Los Angeles have often been in the forefront of campaigns in support of tough new laws against the "street terrorism" of Black teenagers in their neighborhoods. And Black celebrities such as Bill Cosby have endorsed the campaigns against the "Bad Black Brother" who is deemed responsible for making the lives of his inner-city neighbors a misery.

These kinds of sentiments have been around on the conservative fringes of both Black and White politics for twenty years. But they have now been greatly strengthened by being subsumed into the mainstream of post-liberal American politics and articulated by leading Black figures.

"Sometimes," Clinton told a Black church congregation in Memphis in November, "all of the answers have to come from the values and the stirrings and the voices that speak to us from within." Old civil rights leaders like Rep. John Lewis of Georgia were as quick as the new Black conservatives to endorse that view:

"The president's speech in Memphis set the tone. I'm sick and tired of people saying they don't have jobs, that they grew up in poverty. I don't care how poor you are, there's no way to justify what's going on in many of these communities."[3]

In the climate created by the distorted race discourse, even somebody like Lewis thus feels it is right to declare himself angry about people *saying* that they don't have jobs and are poor, rather than being angry about the *realities* of desperate poverty and mass unemployment in the inner cities.

In an even more remarkable development, the arguments about accepting individual responsibility instead of criticizing society have been echoed by prominent figures from the radical end of the spectrum of Black opinion. The Reverend Jesse Jackson, for instance, raised some familiar-sounding arguments in a little-reported speech he delivered in June, 1993:

"I know what's wrong. We've gotten to Canaan, and we're free and foolish...We know that you ought to raise the babies you make, we know better! You know that you have to go to school, you know better!...You know you ought to make your neighborhood safe, you know better! . . . You shouldn't rape anybody, you know better! We know better!

"Thirty years ago we prayed to God . . . we prayed to God to be protected by law . . . And here we are, thirty years later, no Bull Connor to stop us now, no George Wallace to stop us now. Thirty years later, no trenches being bombed, thirty years later, no Klan threatening us. We lost more lives through dope than we ever lost to the rope!

"Thirty years later, we're not threatened by someone wearing a White sheet and a hood. We're threatened by a brother, who is a hood living in the hood."[4]

Rush Limbaugh commented, "He not only sounds like the old Jesse Jackson, he sounds like me!" Limbaugh's endorsement bears powerful testimony to the extent to which the Blacklash has taken hold of radical Black opinion. In the era of the post-liberal consensus, the agenda of individual responsibility set on high by the conservative elites of American society has permeated so deeply into the nation's intellectual life that it even sets the tone of Jesse Jackson's firebrand speeches.

THE BIG PICTURE

The sort of argument and initiatives associated with the Blacklash can have an obvious and understandable appeal to many ordinary Black people living in the inner city. After all, these people often experience the brutality of life in these areas through the anti-social behavior of those who leech off of their neighborhoods—the pimps, the pushers, the hardcore gang-bangers, and so on. It must often seem to inner-city residents as if people like these are a primary cause of the misery and suffering that afflicts their districts. It is hardly surprising that the argument that Black America needs to stop blaming others and put its own house in order should therefore find a ready hearing among some members of the community.

By turning its gaze inward on to the Black community, however, this whole approach is ignoring the bigger picture. And because it adopts that misguidedly narrow and insular perspective, it is missing the point about the wider social context in which the local problems of inner city areas arise. Above all, it is missing the key point: that these local problems are often only the *symptoms*, rather than the *causes*, of the biggest barriers confronting Blacks in America.

No doubt gangbangers are guilty of many things. But they didn't create the ghetto; in many ways, it created them. Drug pushers and pimps leech off the poor and the powerless. But they did not institutionalize poverty in the inner cities; they just exploit its consequences.

The petty criminals and anti-social elements of the ghetto did not invent narcotics or the art of the rip-off. Big business did that for them. Nor did they make violence an integral part of American life. This surely has a lot more to do with those who wield power at the top of American society, who have taught us all that the way to solve every problem from a labor dispute to an argument with third world regimes is through the use of massive force.

The trend towards increasingly repressive policing in inner-city Los Angeles did not begin in response to the growth of the Crips and the Bloods. It began long before that, with the identification of all Black people as potential criminals by the authorities. And, as we have seen, under cover of their "war on drugs," the police and legal authorities are now criminalizing entire generations of Black and Latino youth.

To develop a Black response that is adequate to cope with the problems would require looking beyond the hood in the hood and asking who is ultimately to blame for the desperate plight of the inner cities. Is it the street corner crack pusher with his little rocks, or the big time politicians and planners who have written off entire neighborhoods as so much rock and rubble? Is it the neighborhood gangs and their feuds, or the city hall gangs who have created ghettos that look like battle-scarred war zones, complete with a police army of occupation?

The all-pervasive problems of the inner cities cannot seriously be seen as products of the moral shortcomings of individual Black youths. They are first and foremost the product of the systemic shortcomings of American society, which has pushed Black communities to the economic and social margins, where they are treated as a law-and-order problem. Those who concentrate instead on the local symptoms of the malaise, and who talk about Black youth and their behavior as the problem in inner cities, ultimately must end up blaming individual Blacks for poverty, violence, and the other tribulations of life in the ghetto. However worthy their intentions, in practice they are putting the manipulative and dangerous message of the conservative elite into the language of the street and the community.

That, of course, explains why exponents of the "Blacklash" can get such a good hearing in the American media and academic circles. They may kid themselves that their new-found reputations rest upon the power of their intellectual case. But the real reason they find favor with the authorities is that they are endorsing the reactionary ideas about Blacks being to blame that have been generated by the political and academic elites around the "underclass" debate. Moreover, they are endorsing those fashionable conservative ideas with the added credibility that comes from being a Black critic of Black criminality.

These Black spokesmen and spokeswomen (many of them former radicals) have turned inward to rail against the "Black underclass" in the inner cities, and effectively to blame impoverished Blacks for their own plight. Watching this process, I am reminded powerfully of the way in which many Black African intellectuals have now swallowed the western perspective on the problems of Africa. Where once they would have accepted without question that Africa had been raped by the White European powers, now they are far from sure if colonialism was such a bad thing after all.

The modern third-world intellectuals tend to look at the state that independent African nations are in today, observe that some things appear worse than they were under the old colonial system, and point the finger of blame at Black Africans themselves. The fact that western financiers have bled Africa dry for debt repayments, while the great powers have propped up corrupt dictators and fought proxy wars across Africa, is forgotten in this flood of self-recrimination.

The tragedy is that, in their preoccupation with the internal deficiencies of Black Africa, the African intellectuals come close to repeating the old arguments of the slavemasters—that Black Africans are not really fit to govern themselves, and things were better when the White European colonialists held sway. The "Blacklash" intellectuals in America, with their own versions of the "Black underclass" theories and their calls for tougher policing in the inner cities, appear to be following a similarly dangerous trail into the intellectual camp of the enemy.

A FATAL COMPROMISE

The "Blacklash" arguments can be posed in an attractively assertive way, as a call on Black people to reject the liberal depiction of them as hapless victims and to stand up for themselves instead. That sounds like good advice; we should surely all respond to our problems as active agents rather than passive victims. But there is a danger here of creating a new climate of SELF-victimization, in which Blacks blame each other for their difficulties and the truly guilty parties in authority are let off the hook.

Taken to its conclusion, a narrow preoccupation with Black criminality and violence can even end up lending some unintentional legitimacy to the treatment which the police and courts hand out to Black men in the ghetto. For instance, listen to what Brenda J. Muhammad, president of the anti-gang organization Mothers of Murdered Sons, had to say about the Rodney King affair in *Newsweek*'s post-riot survey:

"We can't trust the police and we can't trust each other. Last year we lost more than 25,000 people on the streets of America... more than 70 percent were Blacks who were killed by other Blacks. When are we going to raise up in arms about that?

"We need this same vigor every day when a Black person has been killed on our streets. But not until we rise up as we have in this particular case will we make a difference. The cheapness of Black life perpetuates the attitudes expressed by the King jury. I feel that what a lot of those jurors were saying is, 'Black folk don't care about Black folk, why should we care about Black folk?'"[5]

Brenda Muhammand's anger at what is happening to Black youth is palpable. Yet in her concern to start an uprising against Black crime, she ends up in effect arguing that the criminal behavior of Blacks in the ghettos is partly responsible for what happened to Rodney King. Which, given his record, is consistent with saying that Rodney King is partly responsible for what happened to Rodney King. This is the argument that the Los Angeles Police Department used all along to justify its officers' acts of brutal repression.

Of course, it is not the intention of people like Brenda Muhummad to lend succor to those who brutalized Rodney King. The point is, however, that any prominent voice joining the inward-looking public "Blacklash" in the current context will inevitably distract attention from the wider issues of racial discrimination and repression. And such voices can quite easily arrive at arguments that will lend legitimacy to the American authorities—the same authorities who are ultimately responsible for so many of the problems facing Blacks in the inner cities.

This appears to be an issue on which there is no scope for compromise with the conservatives, be they Black or White. In relation to the inner cities in particular, the modern cult of individual responsibility is solely about blaming the behavior of impoverished communities for their own problems and letting the authorities off the hook. One problem today, however, is that even those Black commentators who remain seriously critical of the conservative case tend to feel obligated to make a concession to the case put forward by the political elites on the issue of individual responsibility. For instance, Cornel West has mounted a trenchant critique of the new Black conservatives, noting how they have fallen "into the trap of blaming Black poor people for their predicament." Yet in seeking to steer a middle course between old-fashioned liberalism and modern conservatism, West seems to have fallen into a trap himself. He ends up joining the attack on what he calls the "more vulgar forms of Black liberalism" for downplaying the personal responsibility of Black people.[6] Others might argue that if only there really were a prominent school of argument espousing such vulgarity today, the conservative elites might not have had matters all their own way in setting the agenda on issues of race, poverty, and social policy.

Nobody pretends for a moment that Black people in the inner cities are perfect little angels, any more than any other section of U.S. society is. But the new cult of individual responsibility that has been sponsored from the White House downwards has nothing, absolutely nothing, to do with addressing the problems of these communities. It has solely to do with shifting responsibility and blame onto the shoulders of poor Black people—and thereby justifying government policies of welfare cuts and militarized policing in the inner cities, while mobilizing White support for these reactionary policies. If that is the case, what is to be gained by honest Black leaders and commentators giving the slightest public credibility to such a moralistic crusade, which can only benefit the elites?

RADICAL BLACK BUSINESS?

Some of the perspectives popular among sections of the Black community today might seem to strike a different tone from the conservative "Blacklash." These alternative perspectives seek to point the finger of blame for the problems of Black people at "White society" in all of its various manifestations. They urge Black people to take a separate stand against the racially biased culture of America and to determine their own future as Blacks.

Such a semi-separatist approach in some ways sounds very different from the conservatism of the "Blacklash" attitudes. Yet beneath the surface, both approaches share some important characteristics. In their different ways, they are responding to the Black experience of segregation and marginalization by turning inward to focus on the Black community itself. As a consequence, even the most radical-sounding Black perspective often ends up adopting a narrowly introspective attitude, the sort that tends to breed conservative and parochial solutions.

The tragedy is that, ultimately, such Black introspection can make it easier for American society to turn its back on Black problems and needs. It can help to endorse the way in which racial inequalities are ignored and Black people ghettoized at the margins of economic and political life in the United States. It can do nothing to confront the central problem of the Black community's enforced position as excluded, second-class citizens in modern America.

We can see an example of how this problem works itself out in relation to proposals currently being put forward by many radical Black organizations and spokespersons. There are various strands of Black nationalism or Black self-determination in circulation in America today. Yet they all appear to be united by their emphasis upon community economic self-development—by which in practice they mean the development of Black business. This approach is presented as distinct and ethnocentric, yet in practice it appears to parallel the prejudiced outlook put forward by the conservative critics of the "underclass"—the argument that what Blacks need is less welfare and more enterprise, so that they can become "successful" Americans.

Everybody from Spike "Malcom X" Lee, through the ghetto rap groups, to the Los Angeles gang leaders now appears to champion notions like Black entrepreneurship and Black business cooperatives as a possible solution to the economic devastation of the inner cities. Their conformist, business-oriented proposals seem to be a far cry indeed from the radical Black alternatives offered in the past. The old revolutionary groups like the Black Panthers certainly meant business; but they meant it in terms of political action, not in terms of dollars, dimes, and cents. Then the radical Black solutions offered had to do with changing the fundamental structures of American society, transforming the way in which the country is run. Now the solutions seem to be more about changing the racial ownership of small businesses in the inner cities.

It is noticeable how many of the Black voices that are the most street-radical, the most anti-establishment, are now also influenced by this conservative emphasis on Black community business. From rap groups to radical film directors, the "Afro-centric" solutions most often offered to the inner city are basically to look inward and develop self-sufficient Black community businesses, ensuring that money generated in the community goes back into the community.

Perhaps the most striking example of how community capitalism now seems to influence all Black perspectives is the attitude that the infamous Crips and Blood gangs adopted in the aftermath of the 1992 Los Angeles riots. Soon after the violence had ended, a coalition of Los Angeles gang leaders issued an unprecedented joint statement on what needed to be done to rejuvenate the ghettos. This was hailed by some as a revolutionary development, and one which should strike fear into the hearts of the city fathers. Yet the most striking thing about the Bloods and Crips' plan is its conservatism.

The central economic demands of the Crips and Bloods were for more assistance for Black businesses in the inner cities. They asked for low-interest loans to be made available to minority entrepreneurs, in exchange for which the new Black and Latino businessmen would have to hire 90 percent of their employees from within the community. The gang leaders also asked for more investment in the community, in return for which they would "request the drug lords of Los Angeles to take their monies and invest them in business and property in Los Angeles."[7]

Aside from this bizarre proposal to turn crack dealers into socially responsible investors, perhaps the most dramatic (and dramatically conservative) proposal in the Bloods and Crips' plan concerned their view of welfare benefits:

"We demand that welfare be completely removed from our community and these welfare programs be replaced by state work and product manufacturing plants that provide the city with certain supplies—The state and federal governments shall commit to expand their institutions to provide work for these former welfare recipients."

That sounds pretty much like "workfare not welfare," a major slogan of the conservative campaign to make the inner-city poor work for their miserly welfare checks. The striking thing about the gangs' proposal for work schemes is that it made no mention of poverty, or of how much people should be paid in government jobs. As such, it seemed to accept the basic premise of the elitist workfare argument: that it is welfare itself, rather than the poverty which it perpetuates, that is the problem in the ghetto.

The fact that an outlaw group like the Los Angeles gang leaders can now publicly support such proposals indicates how far the "enterprise culture" of bringing business ethics into the community and reactionary notions about the welfare "underclass" now influence all manner of Black perspectives. That is a significant and worrying sign of how the elite's manipulative, upside-down presentation of race-related issues has come to influence every aspect of the debate.

WHO BENEFITS?

The impact that the distortion of the race discourse has had within the Black community is not simply an intellectual problem. It has important practical consequences. It means that the energies of the community are being wasted in pursuing introspective business "solutions" that cannot really solve the problems of poverty and deprivation, because they are not even addressing the major America-wide issues of social segregation and institutionalized discrimination. And when those "community" solutions fail, it means that the blame attaches to the Black poor themselves, rather than to the elites that are responsible for the creation of the ghetto.

Even if it were possible to get more Black entrepreneurs going in the ghetto, this step could not improve the standing of the majority of Black people in American society. The promotion of a few more Black businesses will not benefit the thousands of Black people living in desperation in the inner cities.

The demand to create some kind of a "Black capitalism" is not new. Nor is such a project the exclusive preserve of Black church ministers and gangbangers. In the past, Black capitalism has been sponsored by far more powerful lobbyists: congressmen, presidents of the United States from Nixon to Reagan, and corporate executives. But what has all this done to improve the lot of the vast majority of Black Americans?

The fact that Black capitalism has been backed by Republican presidents and other powerful figures who are not normally thought of as friends of the oppressed and underprivileged should itself set the warning bells ringing. These people have supported Black business, not as a means of achieving genuine equality, but as a way to avoid trying to integrate Blacks into the mainstream American economy. The effect has been largely to reinforce the ghettoization of Blacks on the economic fringes.

After the inner-city uprising of the sixties, for instance, corporate interests made a considerable show of supporting Black business in Los Angeles. For example, a subsidiary of General Tire and Rubber Company set up Watts Manufacturing, an independent, Black-run company. The Chrysler Corporation went considerably further, depositing more than one million dollars in the Black-owned Bank of Finance in Los Angeles to help stimulate Black capitalism. Initiatives like these certainly helped industrial corporations to offset pressure to integrate Blacks fully into their core businesses. The benefits that the Black community have gained are far more questionable.

Despite all of the fuss about promoting Black capitalism over the past 25 years, the number of Black-owned businesses in America today remains disproportionately small. This is just one more reflection of how a process of discrimination operates right across the economic board. For example, Blacks have frequently been denied access to the sort of credit finance that would enable them to set up in business for themselves. Whole inner-city districts have effectively been Blacklisted by many banks. But even in the unlikely event that more Black businessmen could get credit, premises, insurance, etc., the promotion of community business offers no way forward for the vast majority of working poor in the inner-cities.

The most recent figures from the census bureau showed that there were around 425,000 Black-owned businesses in the United States, less than 2.5 percent of the country's total enterprises. The vast majority are local concerns, dealing with a Black clientele and taking average annual receipts of around $50,000. Most tellingly, almost 85 percent of Black businesses were one-person enterprises or family firms with NO paid employees at all.[8] In cities like Los Angeles, Black business has remained entrenched in individual entrepreneurship and very small outlets, generating little wealth and no substantial employment prospects. More of this sort of petty hustling seems unlikely to turn things around in the economic wastelands of the inner cities.

The demand for Black community business may sound like a positive step towards self-determination. But in a technological age of global economic relations, the future of millions of Black Americans cannot lie in attempts to create small-scale, village-style community economies isolated in the inner cities. Indeed, the problem seems to be precisely the opposite: it is the way in which Blacks are systematically denied entry into the wider economy, and access to the plentiful resources of society, that needs to be addressed. And it is precisely that issue which the powerful business and political elites would rather keep off the agenda. No wonder they are so happy to have radical Black leaders singing the praises of community enterprise.

All that the promotion of Black community business in the ghetto could really mean would be the arrival of some more family stores and one-man service enterprises in the ghettos, with maybe a few sweatshop workshops and fast-food franchises, owned by Blacks and employing Black labor at minimum wages. At "best," it could mean Blacks replacing Koreans as the storekeepers of an inner-city district like South Central Los Angeles. And what difference would that make to the state of the community?

For young Blacks who are now faced with a life of unemployment, it could provide nothing more than a few opportunities to stand in line for a store assistant's job paying a handful of dollars. The fact that those few dollars were being handed out by a Black entrepreneur, or a Black manager of a state-financed workfare scheme, would seem little cause for celebration. And the notion that these same deprived Black youths could use the framework of community enterprise to become rich themselves is simply ridiculous. No doubt there could be some Black business success stories, some entrepreneurs and employers who make good in the ghetto. But there is only room for a few storekeepers, let alone "self-made" millionaires, at the top of the pile of poverty that is the inner cities of America. The harsh fact is that, for the vast majority of Black people, changing the color of the faces that front small businesses and shops in the ghetto would make no more difference than it did when they changed the color of the faces of some of America's mayors and police chiefs.

Far from providing a solution, the introspective emphasis on developing Black community business can even help to make things worse, by intensifying the isolation and marginalization of Black communities. It allows the authorities to get off the hook for what they have done to those communities, by throwing Black people a few token scraps and telling them to be enterprising and solve their own problems.   And it can endorse the dangerous notion that Black people's problems are somehow separate from those of the rest of American society, and can therefore be solved internally.

The Black communities of the inner-city ghettos will not be rescued from deprivation by attempts to create little self-sufficient village-style economies. On the contrary, they need to be properly incorporated into the wider American economy to get access to the scale of resources required. The presidential election campaign of 1992 revealed the extent to which, in the midst of recession, the American dream of entrepreneurial success has died for many of its erstwhile supporters among White voters. It is thus a cruel irony that, at the same moment, some former Black radicals should be seeking to rekindle belief in their own illusory version of the American dream among impoverished Blacks.

How can we explain this state of affairs? Why should most of the influential Black perspectives today be shaped by such narrow and conservative ideas as those of the "Blacklash" or the community business culture? At least part of the answer lies in the way that the small Black middle class has come to exercise a disproportionate and often overbearing influence on Black politics in the nineties. The rise of the new Black middle class and its narrow concerns is in many ways the flipside of the elite's campaign against the "underclass" and the politicization of the racial divide.

In their concern to gain respectability in the eyes of official America, many of the spokespersons of the Black middle classes have gone out of their way to distance themselves from the Black poor, branded the "underclass." They have proved willing to echo the ruling elite's messages about individual responsibility, crime, and enterprise, as a sign that they are qualified to be considered as decent Americans, on the "right" side of the divide in American society. The consequence is that the Black middle classes have become the mouthpiece for elite ideologies within the Black community, and the policies and responses which that community identifies with have been twisted to suit their narrow, sectional interests.

REPRESSION AND REFORM

In mainstream discussions that relate to the situation of Black Americans today, there is currently a lot of talk about the negative "legacies of the sixties." The poverty and problems of Blacks in the inner cities are often explained away, not as a creation of contemporary American society, but as a consequence of the welfarist policies and attitudes that the 1960s endorsed. In the midst of all this sixties-baiting, however, one real consequence of what began in that decade has often been ignored—that is, the distortion of Black perspectives that has been brought about by the emergence of a small, but loud, Black middle class. That Black middle class and its disproportionate influence over Black politics are both primarily the products of government policies developed in response to the Black revolt of the sixties.

Before the era of civil rights, the Black middle class barely existed outside of clergymen and teachers. Yet these few "respectable" people were very influential in the Black community. When the popular protests for civil rights began in earnest in the 1950s, they were largely respectable affairs led by the Reverend Martin Luther King Jr. and his Southern Christian Leadership Conference.

In 1963, King led the massive freedom march on Washington to demand civil rights for American Blacks. His aim was to galvanize the liberal conscience of White America and rally enough support to push a civil rights bill through congress. Unfortunately for King, much of White America had little or no liberal conscience. As peaceful protests were met with indifference—or with baseball bats and guns—hostility emerged among some civil rights activists to King's deliberately moderate strategy. Even when a civil rights bill was finally passed in 1964, its paper promises made no difference in practice to the vast majority of poor Blacks still suffering racial discrimination. Anger continued to rise in the inner cities. After King was assassinated, it was clear that the focus of the fight for Black rights was about to shift from the passive protest of the southern middle class to the violent revolt of the Black urban working class.

There is a long history of race riots in the United States. Before and after the First World War, and on the largest scale in Detroit in 1943, racists have violently opposed the housing, promotion, or granting of any rights to Blacks. But when violence again spilled onto the the streets of the United States in the sixties—first in Harlem in 1964, then in nine cities in 1965, 38 in 1966, and 128 in 1967—it was Black people on the offensive, hitting back.

Growing confidence on the street was matched inside the factories, as militant Black workers' organizations sprang up in major plants. Black militancy reached perhaps its highest form in the Black Panthers, founded in October 1966, by Huey P. Newton and Bobby Seale. The Panthers organized militant defense of the ghettos and were forced to engage in armed conflict with the police and the FBI.

At a time when U.S. involvement in Vietnam was already taking a heavy economic and political toll, the American authorities had to move fast to halt the Black rebellion in the inner cities. The man called in to reorganize things was Otto Kerner, governor of Illinois, who was put at the head of the Special Advisory Commission on Civil Disorder. The containment strategy that the government built around the Kerner Commission had two distinct strands: to hammer the militants and to integrate a new generation of "respectable" Black leaders.

While Kerner deliberated on the social causes of the riots, the police set out deliberately to crush those Blacks who had proved willing to stand up and fight for their rights. The Black Panthers were first portrayed as violent criminals in an attempt to isolate them from support in the Black community. Then they were ruthlessly put down. Many were assassinated by the FBI in carefully staged shoot-outs. In the riots that followed King's murder, more than 60,000 police and troops killed 38 Blacks and arrested 15,000.

When the Kerner Commission reported, it recommended a major increase in spending on the criminal justice system—the-law-and-order machine—and a shake-up in police organization to improve that machine's repressive efficiency. But when the clouds of smoke and CS gas cleared over America's cities, Kerner and Co. also realized that liquidating Black militants was not going to be enough. If conditions in the ghettos remained unchanged, another generation of Black rebels would replace the Panthers. Kerner even conceded that the riots were, "in large part the culmination of 300 years of racial prejudice." He proposed a series of concessions to American Blacks:

- Recruitment of Black cops—whose "insight" could aid "early anticipation of the tensions and grievances that can lead to disorders";

- A community-relations service program—which set up co-ops, job creation, and training schemes to keep Black youth off the streets;
- Aid for Black businesses—a theme taken up by Richard Nixon in his 1968 program for "minority business enterprise."[9]

Following in Kerner's wake came laws designed to enforce the civil rights legislation. The best-known measure was the introduction of "affirmative action"—quotas for the number of places open to Blacks in jobs and education.

The view has been widely promoted that as a result of the rapid and positive response by the authorities to the riots, Blacks took their rightful place in American society. The reality is different. Politicians like Jesse Jackson and David Dinkins symbolize the most successful aspect of America's response to the riots of the sixties. The authorities have cultivated a layer of middle-class representatives of the Black community who have played a key role in containing Black protests within the safe confines of the political mainstream. They have promoted voter registration drives to persuade Blacks to take their place in the system. There are now thousands of elected Black officials in the United States, and Black mayors have run all six of the biggest American cities.

The affirmative action legislation helped to foster the emergence of a Black middle class. Government agencies rapidly recruited and promoted Blacks and insisted that firms with state contracts —which means most big companies—introduce similar policies. The fact that the U.S. economy was still expanding until the mid-seventies created some scope for the growth in the numbers of Black businessmen and professionals. Yet affirmative action made little difference to the vast majority of working Blacks. More subtle and discreet forms of discrimination persisted. Black unemployment has remained at two to three times the level for Whites, and Blacks are three times more likely to be living below the poverty line.

Since the eighties, the recession and the Reagan-Bush assault have helped to reverse most of the token action in favor of Blacks. Impoverished Black people in the inner cities have borne the brunt of welfare and educational budget cuts. The White House, Justice Department, and Supreme Court have together waged war on civil rights legislation, quotas, and affirmative action.

Today, there are more Black politicians, government officials generals, and police chiefs than ever before. Yet none of this has changed the way in which the state machinery treats ordinary Black people. They have continued to be brutalized by the police and courts, and treated with contempt by the authorities. One of the most dramatic illustrations of police terror under the auspices of Black representatives came in 1985 in Philadelphia, when Black mayor Wilson Goode authorized the paramilitary police to firebomb an entire Black neighborhood in an attempt to evict a small Black religious sect. Eleven Blacks, including four children, were burned to death. Los Angeles Police Chief Darryl Gates declared himself mightily impressed by the Philadelphia action.

The persistence of police repression and the deterioration of the social position of most Blacks confirm that racial oppression in America continues. The relative rarity of riots in Black ghettos in the United States does not mean that racism has been eliminated by the Kerner measures. It shows instead that Black resistance has been largely contained, through a subtle blend of integration and terror.

The consequence of this is that while many thousands of Black people have been hammered further down toward the bottom of American society, a small Black middle class has attained a position of some prominence. The absence of any grassroots Black movement since the sixties has allowed the new generation of middle class Black politicians and intellectuals to appoint themselves as the exclusive spokespersons of

Black America, establishing a pervasive influence over Black politics in the eighties and nineties.

STUCK IN THE MIDDLE

The influence that the Black middle class exerts upon Black public opinion today goes some way towards explaining the problematic Black perspectives that we have examined above. The politics of the "Blacklash" and of Black community capitalism reflect, above all, the concerns and ambitions of this thin layer of society, through which the dominant ideologies of American society are filtered into the Black community.

For example, the acceptance of the notion that impoverished Blacks must carry the blame for their own problems is part of the Black middle class's campaign for respectability. Black professionals want to distance themselves from the brutality of the ghetto and to demonstrate that at least some Blacks are capable of acting as decent and responsible Americans. Taking a stand on the side of law and order and against the criminality of the "Black underclass" is one way that they seek to do so.

Similarly, the advocacy of Black business is also a key concern of the Black middle classes. It will do little or nothing to benefit the vast majority of Black people in the inner cities. But it will provide more opportunities for the minority of middle-class Blacks to consolidate their position in the business community.

The politics of the Black middle class can thus only help to further isolate and marginalize thousands of Black people in America's inner cities. It is high time that Black America broke free of the influence of this manipulative minority and sought out a political perspective that can serve the interests of the majority.

Under the Clinton administration, the disparity between the interests of the Black middle class and the majority of working and poor Black people has become clearer still. While more prominent members of the Black and minority communities are ushered into the corridors of power under the Clinton doctrine of diversity, those branded the "underclass" suffer more militarized policing and cuts in social spending in the inner cities. The new Black politicos and operators need only to look out of their office windows to see an army of Black beggars being controlled by a police army on the streets of Washington. They are that close; but in terms of their needs and aspirations, those at the top and the bottom of Black America are farther apart than ever.

The way in which the sectional concerns of the Black middle class have helped to affirm the political ghettoization of the mass of Black people, has been confirmed by the results of racial redistricting. For some time, aspirant Black politicians pushed to have electoral wars redrawn along racial and ethnic lines to help ensure that Black voters could elect Black representatives. With the support of the authorities, this policy has been widely implemented in recent years, resulting in some bizarre electoral boundaries being drawn along highways to incorporate pockets of Blacks or Latinos in a racial or ethnic constituency. Who has benefited?

Individual Black politicians have reaped the fruits of redistricting in the form of certain electoral victory and a new career. But for the future of the Black community as a whole, the results have been a disaster. Redistricting has formalized the racial divide in American politics. According to one report, in the congressional elections of November 1994 in the South, redistricting "helped both Blacks and Republicans" to get elected.[10]

A few more Black careerists might get into Congress. But redistricting leaves the urban Black communities stuck on the margins of America's political life, ghettoized, and perfectly set up as scapegoats against which right-wing racists can mobilize the fears of White suburban voters. Little wonder that the conservative elites were so willing to give into radical Black demands for redistricting. Such "anti-racist" segregation policies can confirm the elites' view that impoverished Black communities are a race apart from the rest of U.S. society more effectively than old-fashioned racial supremacist rhetoric could ever hope to do in the 1990s.

7. TURNING THINGS AROUND

This book has tried to identify what is in many ways the most dangerous problem confronting people living in the United States of America today. The issues raised and discussed in these few pages are of wider importance than may be apparent at first glance. All of the key questions that touch upon race and racial thinking are not simply of sectional or communal interests. Far from it. The most fundamental matters of freedom and justice in America, questions about the unity of the nation itself, are on the line in the arguments over how the race question might be resolved in these times. The divisive manipulations of racial issues have distorted every discussion about social policy, policing, poverty, and rights in contemporary America.

Racial tensions are now more evident and politically important than they have been in living memory. Yet there is also less effective opposition today to the manipulation of racial divisions and to the ideological onslaught against the Black poor. So what can be done about it all?

There is no single, straightforward, overnight solution to the crisis of race relations in America or to the dire problems facing people in the ghetto. That, of course, has been said many times before, by every politician, pundit, or businessman who is asked to come up with an answer. It is true. But the reasons why it is true are not those which are usually stated.

For one thing, the reason there is no simple solution has nothing to do with a strange, ephemeral phenomenon known as "human nature." Human nature is often cited these days as a reason why a semblance of racial harmony cannot be created in America, or even as an explanation of why so many Blacks suffer in poverty. We are told that it is human nature for Whites to mistrust Blacks, or that it is human nature that makes poor Blacks prefer the world of welfare to that of work—"It is their nature, these people are just like that."

But people are not born with genes which determine that they will be a poor man or woman. When Franz Fanon said in his book *The Wretched of the Earth*, "I am rich because I am White, I am poor because I am Black," he was talking not about natural differences but about the huge disparities in wealth and facilities available to the races in colonial societies. Nor are people born with racial prejudice in their blood and bones. These social evils are the creation of human society, not human nature. They are the products of political and economic organization and action. As such, there seems no rational reason why they cannot be challenged through political and economic action of another kind. Nobody needs think it will be easy, but it is certainly not to be dismissed as "unnatural."

Another reason we are always told that there can be no simple solution for the inner cities is that America does not have the money today to invest in improving the conditions of these communities. This is just so much rot. Of course, the authorities can produce some very impressive figures to show that they have already created a budget deficit of $500 billion a year. But does that paper figure prove that there is no wealth in America, the richest country on earth?

Does the financial plight of New York City mean that there is no money around in the city of Wall Street? Does the fact that California is close to bankruptcy mean that there are no resources left in Los Angeles, a city bursting at the seams with fabulous fortunes? Or is it rather that so much of the huge wealth of America is being wasted and inefficiently spent, leaving too little for such admittedly small matters as saving the lives of the inner-city communities? As Mike Davis has noted, the $2 trillion America spent on "winning" the Cold War and bailing out the savings and loan industry could already have created a very different reality: "Spent on cities and human resources, these immense sums would have remade urban America into the land of Oz, instead of the wasteland it has become."[1]

The major reason there truly is no simple solution has nothing to do with human nature or with a shortage of wealth. It is because dealing with the racial divide and the crisis facing Black America today involves a fundamental challenge to many practices institutionalized in the American system. And before that can be attempted, preparing the ground for such a challenge will require a mighty political struggle—a battle to turn every one of the most powerful perceptions and beliefs about race and poverty in the United States completely on its head.

SOCIAL INVESTMENT

It is high time that consideration shifted from rhetorical attempts to explain away Black poverty to practical attempts to abolish it. The deeply embedded structures of discrimination and segregation need to be taken apart, starting at the top and working downwards. The marginalization of the Black inner-city communities on the fringes of American society needs to be countered, so that these people can play a full part in the country's economic life. This will require some fundamental changes in the way that U.S. society organizes the production and distribution of its resources. There is no scope here to launch into a detailed discussion about how to address these broader structural problems of American society. But it is not difficult to suggest a few modest measures, which could be seen as small steps towards a better use of the wealth which already exits in the United States.

The key question is social investment. The poor need more. And nobody should accept the argument that there are no resources to spare for addressing this problem. The United States of America is awash with wealth, the richest nation history has ever produced. Government statistics can show how serious the budget deficit is, but they cannot alter the bottom line: there is no shortage of human, material, or financial resources in America. However, there *is* an unjust and inefficient system of concentrating control over that wealth in the wrong hands, and for the wrong purposes.

American society needs to provide the impoverished inner-city communities with real work, in order to carry out the vital job of reconstruction. Let there be no confusion here; we are not talking about another proposal for workfare. The workfare schemes all begin from the same basic assumption that the big problem with unemployment is its moral-psychological impact upon the individual. Therefore, supporters of workfare say, what is needed is to get the jobless working in some fashion—even if the "job" only means doing pointless tasks in return for their miserable welfare checks. That is an insult.

In reality, the main problem with mass unemployment in the inner cities is the poverty it creates and re-creates. Nor is poverty only a problem for the unemployed; the fact is that many people with jobs, especially women who support families alone, earn wages BELOW the miserly official poverty line. One-half of working Black mothers are in this miserable group. What good will the moral coercion of workfare schemes do for them?

What people need are jobs that pay a proper wage, enough to raise their families in decent circumstances, not hovering around the official subsistence-level poverty line. And there are plenty of proper jobs that need to be done in the cities—not on some penny-pinching training scheme, but as part of a comprehensive, multi-billion dollar program designed to rebuild the urban heart of American society. Initiating such a program, and in the process creating thousands of jobs at a proper wage, is the first step the American government should take.

But where is the money to come from, ask the bean-counting critics? Let us leave aside for now the central question of a fundamental change in the pattern of wealth creation and distribution in the United States. A few minutes of thought could produce plenty of far more modest measures that might be introduced to raise the resources for an emergency reconstruction program.

After all, two planks of government spending policy during the Reagan and Bush years that helped create the huge government deficit in the first place were tax cuts for the wealthy and massive spending on defense. The consequence of prioritizing these policies was to reduce investment in social programs. In real terms, spending on welfare has been slashed over the past 20 years. Billion-dollar cuts in federal support to local government, meanwhile, have also played a major part in creating the crises of city finance, leading to service and construction cut-backs, layoffs, and more misery from Los Angeles to New York. It is high time for a change in these priorities. There are other spending programs ripe for cutting, and gaping tax concessions ready to be filled, that can generate some investment dollars for reconstruction.

Once the argument for a change in priorities is won, even a moderate reformer can find plenty of likely targets. A few possible savings are worth mentioning here, not as a blueprint, but as a small example of what you can come up with once a little imagination is applied. For example, we could (and most certainly should) de-escalate the war on drugs, while diverting some funds now spent on useless interdiction programs to treatment programs; that would save several billion dollars a year. Even squeezing the corporate rich very gently through taxation would raise enormous resources for redevelopment; for example, it has been estimated that simply by cutting the entertainment tax deduction to 50 percent, the government could raise another $16 billion over five years.

There are some slightly more ambitious targets that come easily to mind as well. After the Cold War, for example, there is an unanswerable case for truly slashing the military budget, from Star Wars downwards. And who is really in favor of America spending an estimated $30 or $40 billion a year on secret funds for the CIA and the rest of what is laughably called "the intelligence community," those patriotic runners of guns and drugs and miners of other people's harbors?

These points are not firm proposals to be incorporated into any detailed economic program. The aim of mentioning them is simply to suggest that there is no shortage of resources, and no shortage of ways to release some of them for a proper jobs-and-rebuilding program. What is missing is the political will to confront the real issues and problems. Those in authority prefer instead to retreat behind their fantastic arguments about "welfare overspending" and the supposed responsibility of a "Black underclass" for wrecking the inner cities.

This brings us to the most immediate problem: that of the current political climate, the post-liberal consensus that we have discussed throughout this book. It is this culture, institutionalized by the political elites, which excuses and legitimizes the continuation of inequality and segregation in U.S. society, and which scapegoats the Black poor for the problems created by the system. If there is to be any hope of taking some practical steps to overcome these problems, the first thing that needs to be done is to alter the terms of the political and intellectual discourse about race in America. Mounting a challenge to the elitist ideologies that now dominate the public debate is the absolute precondition for changing anything in the inner cities themselves. "Today," as one contribution has argued, "a contest rages over the meaning of racism."[2] Scoring some points in that political contest will be the first step towards defeating the divisive and scapegoating war against the Black poor.

NO SHORT CUTS

What kind of political challenge to the existing climate is required? One of the first things that needs to be done is to recognize the extent and the depth of the problem that we are trying to solve. Inequality remains institutionalized at the very heart of American society. It is perpetuated by the leading governmental and corporate elites in the country. The politics of race is not the property of a few outspokenly right-wing congressmen or talk-show hosts. All of the leading political parties and programs have become imbued with dangerous racial attitudes in recent years. As we have seen, the prejudices of Republican conservatives have been translated into the philosophy of the post-liberal mainstream of the Clinton era.

If we are able to come to terms with the extent of the problem, it surely follows that there is no short-cut solution, no easy way around it. The sort of partial reforms and marginal changes that are the stuff of conventional American politics are not going to be sufficient to cope with the ingrained problems of racial division and discrimination. Instead, what needs to be worked towards is a more fundamental challenge to the established forms and norms of social organization. This challenge will need to involve a critical examination of the ways in which wealth is produced and distributed, and of the mechanisms through which political and civil rights are granted and exercised, in the modern nation of America. An essay on the politics of race is not the place to digress into these wider social issues and analyses. But it is important that we flag them here as being pertinent to the discussion of any solution, in order to avoid any temptation to ghettoize the race question as a separate issue, which needs not touch upon other matters of American politics.

Setting up such a demand for change can obviously appear to be a daunting prospect, especially in these essentially conservative times. It is much more attractive to look for partial measures, such as changes to convention or legal reforms, that might at least seem like practical steps in the right direction.

Obviously, anything which improves the situation one iota should be endorsed and embraced by those of a progressive mind, however small a measure it might be. The problem is, however, that too many of the recent proposals that fall into this category have not improved things one iota. Indeed, some of the proposed solutions have only helped to reinforce the problems confronting Black people in America in the nineties. This is because the manipulation of race by the elites has created far more significant problems than a few reactionary slogans and notions can address. It has created a pervasive political climate, an overall atmosphere, which has in turn confirmed a set of attitudes and some unwritten but firm rules of discussion. As a result, any isolated idea or argument that is raised is in danger of being subsumed into the new politics of race and reinterpreted from that standpoint.

This is a very dangerous development, and all the more so if it is not fully understood. It means that ostensibly progressive proposals or initiatives, which may seem worthy of support in their own right, can often be turned into something entirely different in the wider context of a post-liberal consensus against the Black poor.

In recent times, various initiatives have been raised that were intended to advance the cause of equality. But because these proposals for partial reform did not directly subvert the wider framework of the politics of race, it has been possible for some of them to be twisted to suit the dictates of the dominant outlook in contemporary political life. As a consequence, they can end up actually reinforcing the tendencies to marginalize and scapegoat impoverished Black communities in the inner cities, thus serving the interests of the elites that they were intended to challenge.

Take, for example, the recent high-profile emphasis upon issues of language and labels. Black intellectuals and academics, in particular, have combined with the "politically correct" lobby in campaigns to ban the use of what they consider to be "offensive" expressions and epithets. So we have seen the advance on campus of such linguistic phenomena as "People of Color" replacing what are seen as more derogatory names. More broadly, corporate and governmental America has largely been willing to endorse new language codes in public life.

The new PC emphasis upon banning offensive language might sound like a good thing from the point of view of ordinary Black people. After all, no section of American society has put up with more abuse than they. And certainly, public figures are no longer as free to engage in blatantly racist remakrs. President Clinton has not—as one of his Democratic predecessors in the White House was infamously said to have done—rung up a major television network during a broadcast from famine-struck Africa, with orders to "get those nigger babies off my TV." The perpetrators of the slightest linguistic indiscretion can now expect to be punished with accusations of racism. When presidential candidate Ross Perot referred to the audience of a National Association for the Advancement of Colored People as "you people," it was sufficient to damage his campaign and damn him in the eyes of most language-sensitive liberals and Black leaders.

However, the campaign against offensive language cannot really be considered a major success from the point of view of the majority of Black people. Worse, it has been reinterpreted within the framework of the war against the Black poor and turned into another argument that holds the "Black underclass" responsible for a problem.

Today, the crusade against offensive language tends to be directed against anything that is considered offensive to the middle-class morality of the new American mainstream. This means that not just openly racist abuse is out. The street language of the ghetto is at least as offensive to the moral guardians of nineties' America. Indeed, since racism is usually expressed in code these days anyway, much of the fuss about offensive language has been focused against the words used by rappers and other Black artists. Typical of this is Tipper Gore's campaign against the "offensive" lyrics of Black ghetto rappers.

The problem of trying to put forward progressive reforms without challenging the broader framework of racial prejudice also recurs again and again in relation to issues of gender. In recent years, for example, Black feminists have become increasingly outspoken against the "macho" lifestyles of many Black males, in particular their unenlightened attitudes towards women and childcare. These arguments often seem liberal and progressive. Yet within the context of the broader post-liberal consensus on race, they can be twisted into something very different.

The attack upon the sexism of the ghetto male can be interpreted as further evidence of how the behavioral problems of the Black "underclass" are responsible for the crisis of inner-city communities. This is a political bonus for the elites, who are only too happy to have feminists unwittingly point the finger at Black stereotypes. Witness the prominence given to those Black feminists who came forward to denounce Mike Tyson as a rapist, and especially to those who attacked O.J. Simpson as a perpetrator of domestic violence.

To point out how these arguments are being twisted today is not to deny the importance of such gender issues. But it is also important to grasp how, so long as the underlying political climate on racial issues stays intact, there remains a constant danger that these discussions will be manipulated into another way of ensuring that the finger of blame for "offensive" behavior gets pointed at Black men from the bottom of American society. Meanwhile, those well-spoken figures in authority at the top of American society, who are responsible for causing and perpetuating many social problems, are not only let off the hook, but are allowed to look down their noses at the foulmouthed niggers who refuse to conform to the civilized language codes adopted in Washington and on the college campus. The truth is once more turned on its head, this time with a liberal twist.

Working out how to balance concerns of gender and race is certainly an important task. In the context of our discussion here, however, there is scope only to emphasize the danger of pursuing a discussion about the individual problem of the Black male without focusing on the broader social causes of racial (and indeed sexual) inequality.

Proposals and initiatives seeking piecemeal changes and reforms have too often been swallowed up by the powerful influence of the politics of race. While it remains important to demand reforms that can bring some immediate benefits (however minor they might be), it ought to be clear that to stand a chance of being effective such demands need to be raised in the broader context of a challenge to the foundations of racial thinking. The precondition for success is to go further than is usual in our conservative times, to pose some more far-reaching questions about American society and its attitudes, and to tackle head-on some of the political conventions of the post-liberal age.

ASK THE EMBARRASSING QUESTIONS

To challenge the political climate means trying to set an independent agenda, that focuses on important issues currently being distorted or ignored. There are some questions which sound obvious enough but which seem to be entirely absent from contemporary political and intellectual debate in America. Let us start to ask them, and do it loudly.

For instance, why should crime and personal morality be treated as burning political issues, while poverty and unemployment are treated as permanent facts of life—and all but ignored?

How can it be that some of the poorest and least powerful communities in the inner cities are held responsible not just for the difficulties that blight their own areas but even for the problems facing the rest of American society?

Why is the continued reality of racial discrimination in the United States treated as if it were a thing of the past, while the kind of social Darwinism that we thought had been buried in the past is increasingly accepted as modern social theory?

What gives the corrupted and discredited elites of American politics and the media the right to sermonize about the morals and behavior of those whom they oppress, and to enforce their will through a police army of occupation?

And if America truly wants to consider itself a democracy, who is to control the destiny of the Black and Latino communities of the inner cities? Is their future to be decided by Washington officials, police chiefs, big-city planners, and newspaper editors? Or are they to gain some sort of control over their own lives, some chance to build a decent future for themselves and their families?

There are many more questions to be posed once the imagination is permitted to range over the largely unexplored terrain of today's pressing issues. There is a need to explore every opportunity, to start to turn some of the twisted conventional wisdoms of today on their heads and put the truth back on its feet.

It needs to be shouted from the rooftops and argued on every doorstep that Black people and their behavior are not the problem facing America. The problems that need to be addressed are the ways that society functions, rather than the ways that Black, Latino, or any other individuals behave because many of these social problems afflict Black people disproportionately.

It is time to start talking openly about race in American politics. It is important that America starts openly discussing the issue of race and the attitudes of those in authority and of wider society towards it. The new politics of race can only be fought out in the open, away from the shadows of innuendo and insinuation.

It is time that all of the ciphers and codes used in American politics were broken. The double-meaning discussions about the problems of crime or welfare or individual responsibility should be exposed for what they really are: largely moralistic attempts to scapegoat the poor, and especially the Black poor, for the problems of the city. The issue of race, and the reality of what Black people put up with in this country, ought to replace these dishonest debates at the center of public affairs.

In this spirit, it is vital, too, that critically minded people should now seek to turn on its head the ever-widening discussion about "the problem of the Black underclass." As argued elsewhere in this book, the real problem is not some behavioral "culture of poverty" but poverty and repression itself among Blacks and Latinos in the inner cities.

Tackling the dire economic circumstances of these communities should be of a paramount importance. In the first place, this action will involve challenging the ideas and the arguments that are routinely used in an effort to explain away Black poverty—primarily the various reactionary theories that center on the existence of a criminal "Black underclass" creating its own problems (and creating most of society's problems too). The first step is to start dismantling the ideological walls that the elites have used to trap many Blacks in poverty and to hold them responsible for the societal malaise. The next step is to come forward with some sort of practical proposals about how this problem might be addressed. But unless the political argument against the manipulation of the race issue has been addressed, and the post-liberal consensus challenged, there can be no hope of putting any such proposals into practice.

When it comes to discussing the economics of inner-city areas, there are powerful misconceptions, planted and watered by the elite ideologists, that need to be torn up by the roots and examined. The biggest of these is the notion that America spends far too much money on its inner-city communities—a notion that powerfully misinforms the current debate about welfare.

The undisputable fact, which should be hammered home at each and every opportunity, is that the people who live in the ghettos get far too little of the wealth and resources of American society. The entire discussion about these Black and Latino communities being pampered on welfare is a bizarre and bitter twisting of the truth. Those who use this argument are guilty of a remarkable feat of intellectual contortionism. They are accusing the poorest sections of American society of enjoying unfair privileges. This strange idea needs to be exposed as a cynical device for protecting those in positions of power, who truly enjoy massive privileges in the allegedly classless society of contemporary America.

There is plenty that the American authorities could do if they were serious about addressing the grievances of the Black poor. But at the same time, the problems are far too serious to be simply handed over to untrustworthy politicians, with our best wishes for a speedy recovery. Waiting for the solution to be handed down from government is the surest guarantee that there will *be* no effective solution to the crisis of race relations in the cities of America. There can be no administrative, colonial-style, top-down solution to the problems confronting Black communities in America. The elites who hold the reins of power have been responsible for institutionalizing and intensifying racial division. It would be naive in the extreme to imagine that they can be entrusted with the task of uniting the nation. It will require a lot of pressure from the bottom upwards before any genuine progress is made in challenging the crisis in race relations. There is a pressing need to work out some new strategies for popular political activity and to organize action towards that end.

FROM THE BOTTOM

There is a challenge for those who see themselves as leaders of the Black community: to develop a new way forward that can relate to the bitter experience of those whom they claim to represent. The question now for Black leaders is, how can the energies and sentiments of their angry constituencies be channelled into a consistent challenge to those who cause the problems?

The typical responses from Black leaders today seem to fall into two equally problematic categories. Either they depict Black people as pathetic victims of White racism, unable to do anything and in need of more protection from the authorities; or they go to the other extreme and, as in the case of the spokesmen of Black conservatism, demand that Black people stop being a burden on society, clean up their own communities, and become self-reliant chasers after the American dream. Neither of these approaches will do for the last few years of the twentieth century.

What is required are Black leaders who can cultivate a balanced outlook—one that says, Yes, Black people are oppressed, but no, we don't have to be victims. An outlook that says, Yes, Black people should develop their sense of self-respect—but in order to stand up and fight back against institutionalized discrimination, not in the forlorn hope of winning favor with the elites, which have built a system to keep them in their place.

The Black communities of the inner cities need to find their voice and make a mark on the political map, where at present they are treated as the objects, rather than the subjects, of action—as people to whom things are done, rather than people who can achieve things for themselves. This poses an important challenge to all those who put themselves forward as leaders of the Black community. Today we need Black leaders who can avoid both of the contemporary traps—conservatism, on the one hand, and victim politics on the other—and create a culture of Black people standing up for themselves in order to change the system that keeps them down.

The future direction of Black leadership is an issue that will need to be examined further. But it is far from the only problem in organizing political action. There is another trap which needs to be avoided—that of exclusively focusing on the politics of the Black community itself. The unavoidable fact is that the solution to racial problems does not lie in the hands of Black people alone. Whatever Black Americans do, they are a minority. The case for change will have to be taken up, and won, in the wider, Whiter American society, if anything substantial is to be achieved.

The habit of exclusively focusing our attention on the Black communities is understandable, given the wider racial climate in America. Yet it can serve to reinforce the isolation of many Black communities from the main body of American society. Of course, the pressure for proper change must come in part from Black people, from Latinos, and from other disadvantaged minorities. They have a key role to play in standing up to discrimination and repression. But however hard they were to fight, Blacks would be unlikely to succeed alone. The Black minority simply does not carry enough weight in American society. The very marginalization against which we are protesting ensures that Black people lack the clout to change things on their own. The Los Angeles riot itself demonstrated the limitations of an outburst of anger from the oppressed minorities. Such a display of lashing-out in fury can shake the system temporarily. But it cannot achieve the sort of permanent, root-and-branch changes required in U.S. society today.

If the pressure from below is to make itself count, it will almost certainly have to involve support from a significant section of the White American population. Ways will have to be found to reach outward, across the racial divide, to challenge those who have politicized the racial divide on their home turf.

Race hatred in America is a social and political construction that has been continually encouraged and exploited by those in power for their own cynical purposes. As such, it can be challenged politically. Of course, there are now many White Americans who will never be won over to the cause of racial equality and justice. They are too steeped in the modern American traditions of racial prejudice and repression. So be it. But there are many others whom Black America would write off at its own peril. Here the emphasis must particularly be on the youth, those who have nothing invested in the busted American dream and everything to fight for in the future.

A CAUSE FOR UNITY

Trying to get young White Americans to take a stand against racial politics will not be easy. But this attempt need not be, as it is often envisaged, an idealistic, utopian appeal to their altruistic instincts. These young people do have real interest in combating racial discrimination and prejudice.

Although Black people inevitably bear the brunt of oppression, racism also has a damaging impact on our whole society. It is divisive, turning us against one another and disaggregating any popular opposition to those elites who control the society in which we live and are responsible for the social problems that we all face. It is demoralizing, since it infuses White communities with reactionary, backward ideas that tie them to the forces of conservatism in American society and help hold back progress on every social issue. And it is degrading, because it ensures that we all have to live in an uncivilized environment, where the forces of law and order can beat a man to a pulp in front of a video camera and still walk the streets as upholders of the American way. Combating the politics of race is a necessity, if we want to live in a world where decency and real democracy prevail.

The task of winning both Black and White Americans over must begin with an ideological battle against the central premises and myths of the post-liberal consensus. In promoting the case for liberation and equality in the nineties, we need to turn things around, to stand the truth back on its feet, by exposing the origins, the myths, and the dangerous consequences of today's racial politics.

The defining feature of racial politics is that such politics do not only discriminate against impoverished Blacks at the bottom of the pile; they also find those people at the bottom guilty of causing their own problems, and some of the major problems of American society today, and so play into the hands of the most privileged and powerful elites. That is the lie of our times which needs most urgently to be overcome.

NOTES

PREFACE

1. Andrew Hacker, "Clinton and the Blacks," *New York Review of Books*, Jan. 28, 1993.

1. A DISTORTED DISCOURSE

1. See Catherine S. Manegold, "Portrait of the Electorate: Who Voted for Whom in the House," *New York Times*, Sunday, November 13, 1994, sec.

2. See Andrew Hacker, *Two Nations: Black and White, Separate, Hostile, Unequal,*(New York: Scribners, 1992), p.94-98.

3. Douglas S. Massey and Nancy A. Denton, *American Apartheid: Segregation and the Making of the Underclass*, (Cambridge,MA: Harvard University Press, 1993)

4. "String 'Em Up," editoral, *The Nation*, November 21, 1994.

5. Kenneth B. Clark, *Dark Ghetto: Dilemmas of Social Power*, (New York: Harper and Row, 1965), p.11.

6. Kerner Commission, "The Kerner Report: The 1968 report of the National Advisory Commission on Civil Disorders," (New York:Pantheon Books,1988) p.1.

7. "The Kerner Report," p.2.

8. See Oscar Lewis, "The Culture of Poverty," in Daniel P. Moynihan (ed.) *On Understanding Poverty: Perspectives from the Social Sciences*, (New York: Basic Books, 1968), pp.187-220.

9. See Charles Murray, *Losing Ground: American Social Policy, 1985-1980*, (New York: Basic Books, 1984), and Lawrence M. Mead, *Beyond Entitlement: The Social Obligations of Citizenship*, (New York: Free Press, 1986).

10. Quoted in Paul Gordon Lauren, *Power and Prejudice: The Politics and Diplomacy of Racial Discrimination*, (Boulder, CO: Westview Press, 1988), p. 55.

11. Richard J. Herrnstein and Charles Murray, *The Bell Curve: Intelligence and Class Structure in American Life*, (New York: Free Press, 1994), p.340.

12. *The Bell Curve*, p.340.

13. The Bell Curve, p.340.

14. *The Bell Curve*, pp.312, 315.

15. See *New Republic*, October 31, 1994.

16. See Theodore W. Allen, *The Invention of the White Race*, Vol. 1 of *Racial Oppression and Social Control*, (New York: Verso, 1994), and David R. Roediger, *Towards the Abolition of Whiteness*, (New York: Verso, 1994).

2. POLITICS OF RACE

1. Fred L. Pincus and Howard J. Ehrlich, "The Study of Ethnic and Race Relations," in Pincus and Ehrlich (eds.), *Race and Ethnic Conflict*, (Boulder, CO: Westview Press, 1994), p.7.

2. *New York Times*, November 11, 1994.

3. Cited in Thomas Byrne Edsall, "Willie Horton's Message," *New York Review of Books*, February 13, 1992.

4. *New York Times*, Sunday, November 27, 1994

5. Stanley B. Greenberg, "Report on Democratic Defection," 1985, cited in Thomas B. Edsall and Mary D. Edsall, *Chain*

Reaction: The Impact of Race, Rights and Taxes on American Politics, (New York: Norton, 1991), p.182.

6. *New York Times*, May 4, 1992

7. A. Lazarowick, *Years in Exile: Liberal Democrats 1950-59*, (New York: Garland 1988), p.42.

8. Massey and Denton, *American Apartheid*, p.42.

9. See Kenneth Jackson, *Crabgrass Frontier: The Suburbanization of the United States*,(New York: Oxford University Press, 1985), pp.195-200.

10. Ibid., p.209.

11. Nathan Straus (ed.), *Two Thirds of a Nation:* , A Housing Program, 1952, (New York:Knopf, 1952) p.229.

12. Massey and Denton, p.57.

13. A. Hirsch, *Making the Second Ghetto*,(New York: Cambridge University Press) pp.252-254.

14. Mike Davis, *City of Quartz: Excavating the Future in Los Angeles*,(New York: Vintage, 1992), p.253.

15. Kevin Phillips, *The Emerging Republican Majority*, (New York: Anchor Books, 1969), pp.68-69.

16. David Schnall, *Ethnicity and Suburban Local Politics*, (New York: Praeger, 1975), p.150.

17. *The Kerner Report*, p.244.

18. Edsall and Edsall, *Chain Reaction*, p.182.

19. Phillips, *The Emerging Republican Majority*, pp.468-470.

20. Garry Wills, *Nixon Agonistes: the Crisis of the Self-Made Man*, (New York: Houghton Mifflin, 1970), p.265.

21. Quoted in William Greider, *Who Will Tell the People?: the Betrayal of American Democracy*, (New York: Touchstone, 1992), p.276.

22. *Los Angeles Times*, August 18, 1992.

23. Ibid.

24. Quoted in Garry Wills, "The Born-Again Republicans," *New York Review of Books*, September 24, 1992.

25. Alan Ehrenhalt, "An Era Ends Silently," *New York Times*, November 1, 1990.

26. *New Democrat*, July 1992.

27. Quoted in Joan Didion, "Eye on the Prize," *New York Review of Books*, September 24, 1992.

28. *New York Times*, November 11, 1994.

29. See James Stimson, *Public Opinion in America: Moods, Cycles and Swings*, (Boulder, CO: Westview Press, 1992).

3. BLAMING BLACKS FOR BEING POOR

1. Rush Limbaugh, *See, I Told You So,*(New York: Pocket Books, 1993), p. 224.

2. Ibid, p.248

3. *New York Times*, May 9, 1992.

4. Michael Omi and Howard Winant, "The LA Riots and Contemporary U.S. Politics, " in Robert Gooding-Williams (ed), *Reading Rodney King: Reading Urban Uprising*, (New York: Routledge, 1993), p. 97.

5. *Los Angeles Times*, May 3, 1992.

6. See, *Newsweek*, April 6, 1992

7. Andrew Hacker, *Two Nations: Black and White, Separate, Unequal*, (New York: Scribners, 1992) p. 94

8. Ibid., p. 98.

9. Quoted in *Newsweek*, March 30, 1992.

10. For tables showing relative under-representation and over-representation of Blacks in various occupations, see Hacker, *Two Nations*, p. 111.

11. See Thomas Sowell's two major works, *Ethnic America*, (New York, Basic Books, 1981), and *Markets and Minorities*, (New York: Basic Books, 1981).

12. Cynthia Hamilton, *Apartheid in an American City: The case of the black community in Los Angeles*, Labor/Community Strategy Center pamphlet, p. 7.

13. See, D. Caraley, "Washington Abandons the City," *Political Science Quarterly* 107:1 (1992).

14. Hacker, *Two Nations*, p.101.

15. *Business Week,* May 18, 1992.

16. Hamilton, *Apartheid in an American City*, p.8.

17. *Business Week*, May 25, 1992.

18. Quoted in *New York Review of Books*, June 11, 1992.

19. Quoted in *Newsweek*, May 11, 1992.

20. From "Menace II Society," directed by Albert and Allen Hughes, 1993.

4. CRIME: IT'S ALWAYS THE BLACK MAN

1. *Newsweek*, December 5, 1992.

2. Quoted in *Time*, May 11, 1992.

3. Massey and Denton, *American Apartheid*, p.77

4. Quoted in *New York Times*, November 25, 1992.

5. *New York Times*, September 16, 1992.

6. *New York Times*, November 6, 1994.

7. Quoted in *Time*, May 11, 1992.

8. Melvin L. Oliver, James H. Johnson Jr., and Walter C. Farrell Jr. "The Verdict and the Rebellion in Retrospect" in Robert Gooding (ed.), *Reading Rodney King*, (New York: Routledge, 1993), p.119.

9. *Time*, May 11, 1992.

10. Details of cases cited in H. Hawkins and R. Thomas, "White policing of black population—A history of race and social control in America," in E. Cashmore and E. MacLaughlin (eds.), *Out of Control? Policing Black People*, (London: Chapman and Hall, 1991.)

11. Quoted in R. Fogelson, *The Los Angeles Riots*, (New York: Arno Press, 1969) and *The New York Times*, 1969, p.320.

12. Quoted in *Los Angeles Times*, March 28, 1988.

13. Mike Davis, *City of Quartz*, p. 253.

14. Quoted in *Los Angeles Times*, April 7, 1989.

15. *Los Angeles Times*, April 22, 1990.

17. Dan Baum, "The Drug War on Civil Liberties," *The Nation*, June 9, 1992.

18. Mike Davis, "Who Killed LA? The War Against the Cities," *Crossroads*, June 1993.

19. *Newsweek,* September 27, 1993.

20. Gary Kleck, *Point Blank: Guns and Violence in America*, (New York: A. de Gruyter,1991), p.5.

21. *New York Times*, May 20, 1992.

22. *Time*, August 2, 1993

23. Quoted in *Newsweek*, December 6, 1993.

5. THE INVENTION OF THE "UNDERCLASS"

1. Pincus and Ehrlich, "The Study of Race and Ethnic Relations, p.4." in *Race and Ethnic Conflict, (Boulder, CO:Westview Press, 1994).*

2. Isabel Sawhill, "The Underclass: An Overview," in *Public Interest*, No.96, p. 3.

3. Paul E. Peterson, "The Urban Underclass and the Poverty Paradox," in Christopher Jencks and Paul E. Peterson, *The Urban Underclass*, (Washington, DC: Brookings Institutions, 1991), p.3.

4. See, Charles Murray, *Losing Ground*, (New York: Basic Books, 1984), and Christopher Jencks, *Rethinking Social Policy: Race, Poverty and the Underclass*, (Cambridge, MA: Harvard University Press, 1992).

5. Charles Murray, "The Legacy of the Sixties," *Commentary*, July 1992, p.30.

6. Isabel Sawhill, "The Underclass: An Overview," in *Public Interest*, No. 96, p.5.

7. Daniel P. Moynihan, "The Tangle in Pathology," quoted in David B. Grusky, *Social Stratification In Sociological Perspective*, (Boulder, CO: Westview Press, 1994), p. 557.

8. Patti Davis, *The Way I See It*, (New York: GP Putnam and Sons,1992), pp.33, 39, 53, 66.

9. Sawhill, "An Overview," p.10.

10. Midge Decter, "How the Rioters Won," *Commentary*, July 1992.

11. Charles Murray, "Underclass: From Liberal Guilt to Awkward Questions," *London Sunday Times*, May 3, 1992.

12. Tim Rutten, "A Different Kind of Riot," *New York Review of Books*, June 11, 1992.

13. William J. Wilson, *The Truly Disadvantaged: the Inner-City, the Underclass and Public Policy*, (Chicago: University of Chicago Press, 1987).

14. Daniel P. Moynihan, "Toward a Post-Industrial Social Policy," *Public Interest* No.96, p.19-20. For an idea of Moynihan's earlier views on the causes and consequences of poverty in the ghetto, see D.P. Moynihan (ed) *On Understanding Poverty*, (New York:Basic Books, 1968).

15. *Newsweek*, December 15, 1993.

16. Quoted in *The Nation*, July 25, 1994.

17. Decter, "How the Rioters Won," p.21.

6. THE BLACK RESPONSE

1. Cited in Ronald T. Takaki, *Violence in the Black Imagination*, (New York: Oxford University Press, 1993), p.4.

2. Cited in M. Decter, "How the Rioters Won."

3. Clinton and Lewis quotations both from *Newsweek*, December 6, 1993.

4. Quoted in R. Limbaugh, *See I Told You So*, (New York: Pocket Books,1993), p.247.

5. *Newsweek*, May 11, 1992.

6. Cornel West, *Race Matters*, (Boston: Beacon Press, 1993), pp.50 and 57.

7. Gangs' statement reprinted in "The LA Rebellion: Message Behind the Madness," *The Source*, August 1992.

8. Census Bureau figures for Black business reprinted in Hacker, *Two Nations*, p.108.

9. See Kerner Commission,"Report of the National Advisroy Commission on Civil Disorder," (New York: Bantam Books, 1968).

10. *The New York Times*, November 11, 1994.

7. TURNING THINGS AROUND

1. Mike Davis, "Who Killed LA? The War Against the Cities," *Crossroads*, June 1993.

2. Bob Blauner, "Talking Past Each Other: Black and White Languages of Race," in Pincus and Ehrlich, *Race and Ethnic Conflicts*, p.20.

BIBLIOGRAPHY

Allen, Robert. *Black Awakening in Capitalist America*. Garden City, N.Y.: Doubleday and Co., Inc., 1969.

Allen, Robert. *Reluctant Reformers; Racism and Social Reform Movements in the United States*. Washington D.C.: Howard University Press, 1974.

Ashmore, Harry. *Civil Rights and Wrongs: A Memoir of Race and Politics 1994-1994*. New York: Pantheon Books, 1994.

Bell, Derrick. *And We Are Not Saved: The Elusive Quest for Racial Justice*. New York: Basic Books, 1987.

Bell, Derrick. *Race, Racism, and American* Law. Boston: Little Brown, 1973.

Bell, Derrick A. *Faces at the Bottom of the Wells: The Permanence of Racism*. New York: Basic Books, 1992.

Blauner, Robert. "Internal Colonialism and Ghetto Revolt." *Social Problems*, 16 (Spring, 1969), 393-408.

Blauner, Robert. *Racial Oppression in America*. New York: Harper & Row, 1972.

Blauner, Robert. *Black Lives, White Lives*. Berkeley, CA: University of California Press, 1989.

Boyd, Herb, and Allen, Robert, eds. *Brotherman: The Odyssey of Black Men In America-An Anthology.* New York: One World/Ballantine, 1995.

Carmines, Edward G, and Stimson, James A. Issue *Evolution: Race and the Transformation of American Politics.* Princeton: Princeton University Press, 1989.

Carnoy, Martin. *Faded Dreams: The Politics and Economics of Race in America.* New York: Cambridge University Press, 1994.

Clark, Kenneth B. *Dark Ghetto: Dilemmas of Social Power.* New York: Harper & Row, 1965.

Choldin, Harvey M. *Looking for the Last Percent: The Controversy Over Census Undercounts.* New Brunswick, NJ :Rutgers University Press.

Cobbs, Price M., and Grier, William. *Black Rage.* New York: Basic Books, 1968.

Conti, Joseph. *Challenging the Civil Rights Establishment: Profiles of a New Black Vanguard.* New York: Praegi Press, 1993.

Cose, Elise. *The Rage of a Privileged Class.* New York: Harpercollins, 1993.

Cruse, Harold. *The Crisis of the Negro Intellectual.* New York: Morrow, 1967.

Cruse, Harold. *Rebellion or Revolution.* New York: William and Co., Inc., 1968.

Cruse, Harold. *Plural but Equal; A Critical Study of Blacks and Minorities and America's Plural Society.* New York: William Morrow, 1987.

Davis, Mike. *City of Quartz.* New York: Vintage Books, 1992.

Dawson, Michael C. *Behind the Mule: Race and Class in AfricanAmerican Politics.* Princeton, New Jersey: Princeton University Press, 1994.

Dyson, Michael Eric. *Making Malcolm: the Myth and Meaning of Malcolm X.* New York: Oxford University Press, 1995.

Edsall, Thomas Byrne, and Edsall, Mary E. *Chain Reaction: The Impact of Race, Rights and Taxes on American Politics.* New York: Norton, 1991.

Farley, John E. *Majority-Minority Relations.* Englewood Cliffs, New Jersey: Prentice Hall, 1982.

Franklin, John Hope. *The Color Line: Legacy for the Twenty-First Century.* Columbia, MO: University of Missouri Press, 1993.

Gibbons, Arnold. *Race, Politics, and the White Media.* Lanham, MD: University of Maryland Press, 1993.

Giovanni, Nikki. *Racism 101.* New York: William Morrow, 1994.

Glasgow, Douglas G. *The Black Underclass: Poverty, Unemployment, and Entrapment of Ghetto Youth.* San Francisco: Jossey-Bass, 1980.

Gooding-Williams, Robert, ed. *Reading Rodney King.* New York: Routledge Inc., 1993.

Gresson, Aaron David. *The Recovery of Race in America.* Minneapolis: University of Minnesota Press, 1995.

Hacker, Andrew. *Two Nations: Black and White, Separate, Hostile and Unequal.* New York: Scribner's, 1992.

Herrnstein, Richard J., and Murray, Charles. *The Bell Curve: Intelligence and Class Structure in American Life.* New York: The Free Press, 1994.

hooks, bell. *Yearning: Race, Gender, and Cultural Politics.* Boston: South End Press, 1990.

Hutchinson, Earl Ofari. *The Assassination of the Black Male Image.* Los Angeles: Middle Passage Press, 1994.

Jaynes, Gerald David, and Williams, Robin N. *A Common Destiny: Blacks and American Society.* Washington D.C.: National Academy of Science Press, 1989.

Jordan, June. *On Call: Political Essays,* South End Press, 1993.

Katz, Michael. *Improving Poor People: The Welfare State, the "Underclass," and Urban Schools as History.* Princeton: Princeton University Press, 1995.

Katz, Michael. *The "Underclass" Debate.* Princeton: Princeton University Press, 1993.

Kelley, Robin D.G. *Cultural Politics, and the Black Working Class.* New York: Free Press, 1994.

Lusane, Clarence. *African Americans at the Crossroads: The Restructuring of Black Leadership and the 1992 Elections.* Boston: South End Press, 1994.

Madhubuti, Haki R., ed. *Why L.A. Happened: Implications of the '92 Los Angeles Rebellion.* Chicago: Third World Press, 1993.

Marable, Manning. *How Capitalism Underdeveloped Black America.* Boston: South End Press, 1983.

Marable, Manning. *Race, Reform, and Rebellion: The Second Reconstruction in Black America, 1945-1982.* New York: 1984.

Masey, D.S., and Denton, N.A. *American Apartheid: Segregation and the Making of the Underclass.* Cambridge: Harvard University Press, 1993.

McCall, Nathan. *Makes Me Wanna Holler: A Young Black Man in America.* New York: Random House, 1994.

McConahay, John B. "Modern Racism, Ambivalence, and the Modern Racism Scale." In John F. Dovido and Samual L.

Gaertner, eds., *Prejudice, Discrimination and Racism: Theory and Research*. New York: Academic Press, 1986.

McPherson, James M. *The Abolitionist Legacy*. Princeton: Princeton University Press, 1995.

McPherson, James M. *The Struggle for Equality*. Princeton: Princeton University Press, 1995.

Medoff, Peter, and Sklar, Holly. *Streets of Hope: The Fall and Rise of Urban Neighborhood*. Boston: South End Press, 1994.

O'Reilly, Kenneth. *Racial Matters: The FBI's Secret File on Black America, 1960-1972*. New York: Free Press, 1989.

Pinkney, Alphonso. *The Myth of Black Progress*. Cambridge: Cambridge University Press, 1984.

Rief, David. *Los Angeles: Capital of the Third World*. New York: Simon & Schuster, 1991.

Sales Jr., William W. *From Civil Rights to Black Liberation: Malcolm X and the Organization of African American Unity*. Boston: South End Press, 1994.

Scuman, Howard, Steech, Charlotte, and Bobo, Laurence. *Racial Attitudes in America*. Cambridge: Harvard University Press, 1985.

Selznick, Gertrude, and Steinberg, Steven. *The Tenacity of Prejudice*. New York: Harper Row, 1969.

Silverman, Charles E. *Crisis in Black and White*. New York: Vintage, 1964.

Sleeper, Jim. *The Closest of Strangers: Liberalism and the Politics of Race in New York*. New York: Norton, 1991.

Sniderman, Paul M., and Piazza, Thomas. *The Scar of Race*. Cambridge: The Belknap Press of Harvard University Press, 1993.

Sowell, Thomas. *Ethnic America: A History*. New York: Basic Books, 1981.

Sowell, Thomas. *Race and Culture: A World View*. New York: Basic Books, 1994.

Tabb, William K. *The Political Economy of the Black Ghetto*. New York: W.W. Norton & Co., Inc., 1970.

Terkel, Studs. *Race: How Blacks and Whites Think and Feel about the American Obsession*. New York: New Press, 1992.

Toure, Kwame, and Hamilton, Charles V. *Black Power: The Politics of Liberation in America*. New York: Vintage Books, 1967.

Warren, Roland L, ed. *Politics and the Ghettos*. New York: Atherton Press, 1969.

West, Cornel. *Prophetic Thought in Postmodern Times*. Maine : Common Courage Press, 1993.

West, Cornel. *Race Matters*. Boston: Beacon Press, 1993.

Wiley, Ralph, *What Black People Should Do Now: Dispatches from Near the Vanguard*. New York: Ballantine Books, 1993.

Wilson, William J. *The Truly Disadvantaged: The Inner City, the Underclass, and Public Policy*. Chicago: Chicago University Press, 1987.

Yetman, Norman R. *Majority and Minority: The Dynamics of Race and Ethnicity in American Life*, 4th ed. Boston: Allyn & Bacon, 1985.

INDEX

A

Affirmative-action, 45, 47-48, 67, 80-81, 176-77
Africa, 162-63
Allen, Theodore, 22
Arkin, Brian, 32-33
Arkin, Valerie, 33

B

Banfield, Edward, 149
Baum, Dan, 115
The Bell Curve: Intelligence and Class Structure in American Life (Murray/Herrnstein), 9, 11-21
Blacklash. *See* Community response
Black Panthers, 174-75
Bradley, Bill, x
Bradley, Tom, 77, 78
Brown, Jerry, 55-56
Buchanan, Pat, 49-52

Bush, George, 26, 47, 48, 49, 50, 51, 52, 65-66
and "war on drugs," 110-17

C

Carjacking, 95-96
Civil rights, 45-46, 174
Clark, Kenneth B., 9
Clinton, Bill
and diversity, xv-xvi, 33, 179
and gun control, 117-21
and individual responsibility, 153, 159
and 1992 presidential election, 26, 48, 49, 52-59
and welfare, 66-67
The Closest of Strangers: Liberalism and the Politics of Race in New York (Sleeper), 91
Cold War, 6, 51, 97
A Community of Self-Reliance (Novak), 149
Comunity response
of entrepreneurship, 165-73

focus of, 155-57
of individual responsibility
    (Blacklash), 156-65
and institutionalized racism,
    155-57, 160-63, 169-73
of middle-class, 172-80
and politics, 155-57
of self-victimization, 163-65
in societal context, 160-63
See also Solutions: Crime
carjacking, 95-96
and Charles Stuart, 98-99
and Cold War ideology, 97
and criminal profiles, 104-5
and Democratic Party, 48-49,
    58-59
and economics, 94-95
and Federal Alternatives to
    State Trial (FAST), 116-17
and gangs, 113-14, 120, 167-68
and gun control, 117-21
and institutionalized racism, 31-
    32, 48-49, 58-59, 89-91, 92-94,
    96-100, 106-10, 111-17, 118-19,
    120-21
and media, 3-4, 56, 90, 96, 97,
    120
policing of, 6, 91-94, 96, 100-103
proactive policing of, 104-10
and Street Terrorism Enforce-
    ment and Prevention Act
    (STEP) (1988), 113
and Susan Smith, 98-99
and underclass, 90, 95, 97, 99,
    118, 120-21
and "war on drugs," 110-17
and Weed and Seed program,
    115-17
See also Community response
Criminal profiles, 104-5

D

Dark Ghetto (Clark), 9
Davis, Mike, 41-42, 107-8, 183
Decter, Midge, 142-43, 154
Delattre, Edwin, 101
Democratic Party
Black support for, 2, 26
and crime, 48-49, 58-59
and ethnicity vs. race, 33-37,
    43-44
and gun control, 117-21
and institutionalized racism, 28,
    43-45, 48-49, 52-59
and 1994 congressional election,
    26, 27
and 1992 presidential election,
    48-59
and Republican agenda, 52-59
and underclass, 48-49
and welfare, 48-49
See also Politics
Denton, Nancy, 37-38, 41, 92
Dependency culture. *See* Pov-
    erty; Welfare
Didion, Joan, 55
Dinkins, David, 176
Diversity, xv-xvi, 33, 179
Drugs
and Los Angeles Police Depart-
    ment, 112-14
and media, 110-11
and "war on drugs," 110-17
Dukakis, Michael, 47

E

Economics
and Black entrepreneurship,
    165-73
and Cold War, 6, 51

of corporate business, 62-64,
72-75, 77-82
and crime, 94-95
and drug abuse, 110-11
and enterprise zones, 82-85
and immigrants, xiii-xiv, 35
and intelligence, 12-17
of *maquiladoras*, 83-84
and racism solutions, 182-87,
193-94
and taxation, 31-32, 45, 58-59,
82-85
and unemployment, 42
and White flight, 30-31, 40-42, 87
See also Poverty; Welfare
Education, 12-14, 17-18, 76
Elections
1994 congressional, 26, 27
1992 presidential, 25-26, 48-59
1988 presidential, 47-48
1972 presidential, 46
1968 presidential, 45-46
See also Democratic Party; Politics; Republican Party;
specific politicians
Elitism. *See* Institutionalized racism; Politics
The Emerging Republican Majority (Phillips), 42, 46
The End of Equality (Kaus),
85-86
Enterprise zones, 82-85

F

FAST. *See* Federal Alternatives
to State Trial
Federal Alternatives to State
Trial (FAST), 116-17
Federal Housing Administra-
tion (FHA), 39-40
Feminism, 190-91

FHA. *See* Federal Housing Administration
Franz, Fanon, 182

G

Gangs, 113-14, 120, 167-68
Gates, Daryl, 106, 108, 109, 112,
113-14, 119, 177. *See also*
Los Angeles Police Department;
Riots
Gates, Henry Louis, 99-100
Gingrich, Newt, 48, 58, 80
Goode, Wilson, 177
Gross, Jane, 32
Gun control, 117-21

H

Hacker, Andrew, 5
Health care, 69, 76
Helms, Jesse, 48
Herrnstein, Richard, 9, 11-21
Hirsch, Arnold, 41
HOLC. *See* Home Owners Loan
Corporation
Holiday, George, 101
Home Owners Loan Corpora-
tion (HOLC), 39
Horton, Willie, 47
Humphrey, Hubert, 45-46

I

Immigrants
and economics, xiii-xiv, 35
and nationalism, 34
and underclass, 144-46
Individual responsibility
and Bill Clinton, 153, 159
Black community response of,
156-65
and poverty, 10-11, 61-68
Institutionalized racism

Black community response to,
    155-57, 160-63, 169-73
and crime, 31-32, 48-49, 58-59,
    89-91, 92-94, 96-100, 106-10,
    111-17, 118-19, 120-21
current discourse on, ix-xviii, 1-7
and Democratic Party, 28, 43-45,
    48-49, 52-59
and individual responsibility,
    10-11, 61-68, 153, 156-65
and inherent intelligence, 9,
    12-21
issue distortions of, 7-9, 191-95
and Jim Crow laws, 40
and media, xi, 3-4, 7, 56, 90, 96,
    97, 110-11, 120, 128, 146-47
and Republican Party, 28, 31-32,
    43-52
and social construct flaws, 21-23
and social policy, 8-12
solutions to, 183, 186-95, 197
and taxation, 31-32, 45, 58-59
and underclass, 3-5, 20-21, 123-
    29, 131-32, 146-47, 154
and welfare, 31-32, 48-49
and White flight, 7-8, 29-33,
    37-45, 87, 124
See also Politics; Poverty; Solu-
    tions
Intelligence, 9, 12-21
Invention of the White Race
    (Allen), 22

J

Jackson, Jesse, 55-56, 159-60, 176
Jencks, Christopher, 130
Jim Crow laws, 40
Johnson, Lyndon, 45-46, 152

K

Kaus, Mickey, 85-86
Kennedy, John, 45-46

Kerner, Otto, 10, 43, 175-76
King, Martin Luther, Jr., 174
King, Rodney, 25-26, 32, 99-100,
    101-2, 108, 163-64. See
also Los Angeles Police Depart-
    ment; Riots
Koreans, 142-47

L

Language, 189-90
Lewis, John, 159
Lewis, Oscar, 10
Limbaugh, Rush, 64-65, 67, 160
Los Angeles Police Department
and Daryl Gates, 106, 108, 109,
    112, 113-14, 119, 177
and Narcotic Enforcement
    Zones, 113-14
and 1992 riots, 25-26, 32, 56, 91,
    108
and Operation HAMMER,
    113-14
proactive policing of, 104-10
and Rodney King, 25-26, 32,
    99-100, 101-2, 108, 163-64
and "war on drugs," 112-14
and William Parker, 104, 105-6,
    108
and Willie Williams, 108-9
Loury, Glen, 158

M

Maquiladoras, 83-84
Massey, Douglas, 37-38, 41, 92
McDuffie, Arthur, 103
Media
and crime, 3-4, 56, 90, 96, 97, 120
and drug abuse, 110-11
and underclass, xi, 7, 128, 146-47
Moynihan, Daniel, 10, 137-38,
    152

Muhammad, Brenda J., 163-64
Murray, Charles, 130, 133, 143-44, 145-46, 148
and inherent intelligence, 9, 11-21, 124
Narcotic Enforcement Zones, 113-14
National Advisory Council on Civil Disorder, 43-44
Nationalism, 34
Nixon, Richard, 45-46
Novak, Michael, 149

O

Operation HAMMER, 113-14

P

Parker, William, 104, 105-6, 108. *See also* Los Angeles Police Department
Perot, Ross, 57, 189
Phillips, Kevin, 42, 46, 47
Police. *See* Crime; Los Angeles Police Department; specific names
Politics
affirmative-action, 45, 47-48, 67, 80-81, 176-77
and Black community response, 155-57
and Black middle-class, 172-80
civil rights, 45-46, 174
and Cold War, 6, 51, 97
and diversity, xv-xvi, 33, 179
and ethnicity vs. race, 33-37, 43-44
gun control, 117-21
1988 presidential election, 47-48
1994 congressional election, 26, 27
1992 presidential election, 25-26, 48-59

1972 presidential election, 46
1968 presidential election, 45-46
and racism denial, 25-26
and racism solutions, 187-91
and underclass, xiv-xv, 8, 30
"war on drugs," 110-17
and White flight, 7-8, 29-33, 37-45, 87, 124
See also Democratic Party; Institutionalized racism; Republican Party; specific politicians
Poverty
and children, 69
and corporate business, 62-64, 72-75, 77-82
and dependency culture, 63, 64-67, 72-79
and education, 76
and enterprise zones, 82-85
and health care, 69, 76
and individual responsibility, 10-11, 61-68
and inequality, 67-72
and labor force, 63, 69-71, 80-82, 86-87
and maquiladoras, 83-84
reality of, 61-64
and relocation, 85-88
and underclass, 20-21, 129-32, 133-36
and War on Poverty, 2-3, 45-46, 73, 76, 152
and welfare, 11, 65-67, 73-77, 85-88
See also Community response; Solutions
Press, Bill, 27

Q

Quayle, Dan, 141, 153

Quotas. *See* Affirmative action

R

Reagan, Nancy, 112, 138-39
Reagan, Ronald, 47, 138-39
and "war on drugs," 110-17
Red-lining, 38-40
Republican Party
and Democratic agenda, 52-59
and ethnicity vs. race, 33, 34, 36, 37, 43-44
and institutionalized racism, 28, 31-32, 43-52
and 1994 congressional election, 26, 27
and 1992 presidential election, 48-52
and religious Right, 49-52
and "war on drugs," 110-17
White support for, 2, 26
See also Politics
Riots, 174-76
Detroit, 1967, 102
Los Angeles, 1992, 25-26, 32, 50, 56, 65, 91, 108
Los Angeles, 1965, 102, 105-6
Miami, 103
See also King, Rodney; Los Angeles Police Department
Roediger, David, 22
Roosevelt, Eleanor, 36
Roosevelt, Franklin Delano, 34, 35, 36, 38-39
Roosevelt, Theodore, 12
Rothstein, Richard, 84

S

Sawhill, Isabel, 133-34, 140
Segregation. *See* White flight
Sexism, 190-91
Shalala, Donna, 153

Sleeper, Jim, 91-92
Smith, Susan, 98-99
Solutions
arguments against, 181-83
Black leadership for, 195-97
and economics, 182-87, 193-94
and institutionalized racism, 183, 186-95, 197
and issue distortions, 191-95
and language, 189-90
political, 187-91
and sexism, 190-91
social investment, 183-87
unity for, 197-98
Sowell, Thomas, 74
Statham, Stan, xiii
STEP. *See* Street Terrorism Enforcement and Prevention Act (1988)
Stimson, James, 58-59
Street Terrorism Enforcement and Prevention Act (STEP) (1988), 113
Stuart, Charles, 98-99

T

Talmadge, Eugene, 36
Taxation
and enterprise zones, 82-85
and institutionalized racism, 31-32, 45, 58-59
Towards the Abolition of Whiteness (Roediger), 22
The Truly Disadvantaged (Wilson), 150

U

Underclass
behavior of, 3-5, 126-27, 132-36
and Bill Clinton, 153

and crime, 90, 95, 97, 99, 118,
120-21
debate of, 3-5, 123-27
defining, 128-29
and Democratic Party, 48-49
families of, 137-42
and immigrants, 144-46
and institutionalized racism,
3-5, 20-21, 123-29, 131-32,
146-47, 154
and Koreans, 142-47
and liberalism, 125-26, 150-54
and media, xi, 7, 128, 146-47
morality of, 147-54
and politics, xiv-xv, 8, 30
and poverty, 20-21, 129-32,
133-36
and White flight, 7-8, 124
See also Community response;
Solutions
*The Unheavenly: The Nature and
Future of our Urban Crisis*
(Banfield), 149

V

VA. *See* Veterans Administration
Veterans Administration (VA),
39

W

Wallace, George, 46
War on Poverty, 2-3, 45-46, 73,
76, 152
Weed and Seed program, 115-17

Welfare
and Bill Clinton, 66-67
and Democratic Party, 48-49
and dependency culture, 63,
64-67, 72-79
and institutionalized racism,
31-32, 48-49
and poverty, 11, 65-67, 73-77,
85-88
West, Cornel, xvii, 165
White flight
and economics, 30-31, 40-42, 87
and Federal Housing Administration (FHA), 39-40
and Home Owners Loan Corporation (HOLC), 39
and institutionalized racism,
7-8, 29-33, 37-45, 87, 124
and red-lining, 38-40
and underclass, 7-8, 124
and Veterans Administration
(VA), 39
Williams, Willie, 108-9. *See also*
Los Angeles Police
Department
Wilson, William Julius, 150-51
Wilson, Woodrow, 34-35
Wolfe, Alan, 19-20
Women, 190-91
The Wretched of the Earth
(Fanon), 182

Y

Yankelovitch, Daniel, 55

KOFI BUENOR HADJOR

Kofi Buenor Hadjor is a faculty member in the Department of Black Studies at the University of California, Santa Barbara. Hadjor has had first-hand experience of African politics as a press aide in the Publicity Secretariat of Kwame Nkrumah's government. He also represented Ghana on the permanent secretariat of the Cairo-based Afro-Asian People's Solidarity Organization. Hadjor's most recent books include: Kwame Nkrumah and Ghana: The Dilemma of Post-Colonial Power, and the Penguin Dictionary of Third World Terms. He is currently coordinating and editing Encyclopedia Africana.

SOUTH END PRESS

South End Press is a nonprofit, collectively-run book publisher with over 175 titles in print. Since our founding in 1977, we have tried to meet the needs of readers who are exploring, or are already committed to, the politics of radical social change.

Our goal is to publish books that encourage critical thinking and constructive action on the key political, cultural, social, economic, and ecological issues shaping life in the United States and in the world. In this way, we hope to give expression to a wide diversity of democratic social movements and to provide an alternative to the products of corporate publishing.

Through the Institute for Social and Cultural Change, South End Press works with other political media projects—Z Magazine; Speak Out!, a speakers bureau; the Publishers Support Project; and the New Liberation News Service—to expand access to information and critical analysis. If you would like a free catalog of South End Press books, please write to us at South End Press, 116 Saint Botolph Street, Boston, MA 02115. Also consider becoming a South End Press member: your $40 annual donation entitles you to two free books and a 40% discount on our entire list.

RELATED TITLES FROM SOUTH END PRESS

Chaos or Community: Seeking Solutions, Not Scapegoats for Bad Economics
    by Holly Sklar
Haiti: Dangerous Crossroads
    edited by NACLA
Global Village or Global Pillage: Economic Reconstruction from the Bottom Up
    by Jeremy Brecher and Tim Costello
African Americans at the Crossroads: The Restructuring of Black Leadership
    by Clarence Lusane